ADMITS AND OFFERS

Prepare, Decide and Win

Aniruddha M S

Chennai • Bangalore

CLEVER FOX PUBLISHING
Chennai, India

Published by CLEVER FOX PUBLISHING 2024
Copyright © Aniruddha M S 2024

All Rights Reserved.
ISBN: 978-93-56487-92-5

This book has been published with all reasonable efforts taken to make the material error-free after the consent of the author. No part of this book shall be used, reproduced in any manner whatsoever without written permission from the author, except in the case of brief quotations embodied in critical articles and reviews.

The Author of this book is solely responsible and liable for its content including but not limited to the views, representations, descriptions, statements, information, opinions and references ["Content"]. The Content of this book shall not constitute or be construed or deemed to reflect the opinion or expression of the Publisher or Editor. Neither the Publisher nor Editor endorse or approve the Content of this book or guarantee the reliability, accuracy or completeness of the Content published herein and do not make any representations or warranties of any kind, express or implied, including but not limited to the implied warranties of merchantability, fitness for a particular purpose. The Publisher and Editor shall not be liable whatsoever for any errors, omissions, whether such errors or omissions result from negligence, accident, or any other cause or claims for loss or damages of any kind, including without limitation, indirect or consequential loss or damage arising out of use, inability to use, or about the reliability, accuracy or sufficiency of the information contained in this book.

Foreword

I am the co-founder of Gocrackit, an IIM Ahmedabad and IIM Bangalore alumni startup that is disrupting the world of personalized mentoring. We connect students and professionals with the relevant industry mentors who in turn help these students and professionals to choose, prepare, and ultimately succeed in their careers with great amount of fulfillment. We have had over 600 mentors work with around 20,000 candidates on a one-on-one basis since inception.

Aniruddha is among my earliest and favorite mentors, who has worked with hundreds of our candidates over more than 7 years. In fact, he was one of the first beneficiaries of our program since we started, using our mock interviews and resume reviews to crack admits to the one- year MBA courses at IIM A, B, and C. I am happy to see him grow in his career and help so many candidates in his broad field of Operations and Supply Chain Management.

Career mentoring is a less explored but rapidly growing field. Candidates, particularly in the early and middle stages of their careers, face multiple situations where they can benefit from advice and mentorship. And this cuts across demographics of the kind of academic institution, corporate organization, region, age, gender, and so on.

This work of Aniruddha is a result of his many engaging sessions with our mentees and otherwise, and precisely the kind of topic that is needed and sought after by them, and the academic institutions that work with us to make their students job ready. This advice works, as is substantiated by Aniruddha's high overall rating on our website (4.5) and his many mentees who have gone on to get multiple jobs of their choice.

I would share this book across my network of client institutions and mentees to use as a ready reference at multiple points of time in their careers. Career development is a non- stop activity, and it helps to have a standard and trusted guide applicable to a wide variety of scenarios. This book is exactly that.

Suhruta

Table of Contents

Foreword .... *iii*

Before We Begin 1
The Purpose of this Book and its Intended Audience 10
The Blueprint of this Book 16
Knowing Yourself 18
Knowing who you are 20
Knowing what you want 24
Frameworks 31
Your Cheat Codes, Your Mentors 33
Roadmapping a Career Journey 37
Role/ Designation Roadmapping 41
Making your roadmap that extra notch effective 44
Understanding Personalities 46
The psyche of a recruiter 48
The psyche of a hiring manager 51
The psyche of a professor reviewing admissions 53
The psyche of an Admissions officer 56

Table of Contents

Selling Yourself **60**
The Art and Science of Selling Yourself 60
Resume 67
LinkedIn Profile 74
Standardized Tests 82
Statement of Purpose/ Cover Letter 87
Application Forms 99
Other Essays 101
Interviews 103
Group Discussions 116
Understanding an Admit **119**
Selecting a school 121
Selecting a Program 139
Negotiating and Selecting an offer **146**
The principles of negotiation 146
Selecting an Offer 159
Conclusion **169**

Works Cited 170

BEFORE WE BEGIN...

> *I have no time to fall ill*
>
> **Bharat Ratna Sir M Visvesvaraya,**
> *on whose birthday (15th September) India celebrates Engineer's Day, when asked about his good health after the ripe old age of 100*

Sir MV, the maker of the state of Modern Mysore and by extension the success story of Bengaluru is one of my all-time heroes. He grew up in very humble beginnings, and as was often the case in early 20th century India, the only way to success and prosperity was through education and hard work.

A true polymath who was entrusted with the task of being the Diwan of two states (Mysore and Pune), he was the architect of such far-reaching and varied schemes like a dam which provides a lifeline of water to 4 modern states, a paper mill, India's first

Hydro Electric Power Project, a bank as well as a polytechnic college. If you are keen to know more about him and his work, his autobiography, <u>Memoirs of my working life</u> is an excellent read.

An avowed workaholic, he was busy working till his very last breath and had drawn a vision as well as an action plan for what India should do after independence, years before we had gained it from the British.

However, I'm often left wondering if he was naturally inclined towards engineering or if circumstances forced him to be one. This is all the more piqued by the number of people around me who have studied engineering but want to have nothing to do with the vocation or profess to have no clue as to why they chose to pursue it in the first place.

In a sense, a premature version of a mid-life crisis.

Recently, I read a book called *The 100 Year Life* by Lynda Gratton and Andrew Scott which talks about preparing as if we would live for a century or more. Among the remarkable things that are common to blue zones, or areas of the world which have a disproportionately large number of centenarians is the concept of not retiring at all, or maybe sustaining semi-retirement for lengthy periods .

Inherent to this is the need to have both the intention and ability to experiment, learn, unlearn, and make peace with successes and especially failures. And, to have a passion towards life that is driven by a purpose beyond personal well-being.

Before We Begin...

For most of us, our careers (interpreted by me as training for work + work itself) are the dominant markers of our identities and influence our worldview. Our workplace is where we spend much of our good years and a significant portion of our hours therein.

Below is a chart I made for a blog on Work-Life balance where I mapped how we spend much of the 24 hours we have at our disposal at different age brackets. At the peak of our physical, emotional, and cognitive abilities (highlighted in yellow), we utilize that time in our careers.

	AGE BRACKET																
	2.5	5	10	15	20	25	30	35	40	45	50	55	60	65	70	75	80
Sleep	12	10	9	8	7.5	7	7	7	7	7	7	6.5	6	6	6	6	6
Work & Commute	0	0	0	0	0	10	12	12	12	12	10	10	6	4	2	0	0
Study/ Read	0	4	8	10	10	2	1	1	1	1	1	1	2	2	2	3	3
Play/ Exercise/ Hobby/ Nap	0	2	1	2	2.5	1	0	0.5	0.5	0.5	1	1	2	3	4	5	5
Time with Family/ Partner/ Kids	6	4	2	1	0.5	2	2.5	2.5	2	2	3	3	4	4	5	5	5
Time with Friends	2	2	2	1	2	0.5	0	0	0.5	0.5	1	1	2	2	2	2	1
Personal Stuff- Grooming/ Meals	4	2	2	2	1.5	1.5	1.5	1	1	1	1	1.5	2	3	3	3	4
	24	24	24	24	24	24	24	24	24	24	24	24	24	24	24	24	24

People have for long had opinions, habits, and institutions built around the start, sustenance, and end of careers. Let us start with the ancient Indian one. We had clearly demarcated the phases of a 100- year life from cradle to grave (surprise-surprise, that number again) into 4 Ashramas or stages, called Brahmacharya (learning), Grihasta (household), Vanaprastha (retirement) and Sanyasa (renunciation).

This was also clearly an advocacy of job specializations that is intertwined with a whole bunch of other social and political issues which I won't get into. It is the harsh truth in our country that until very recently (say 80 years ago), a choice of career and consequently the course of study to prepare for it was largely determined by two things; the individual's gender and the family he or she was born into.

Much of the workforce was involved in agriculture and that too with small land holdings. As a norm, the firstborn inherited the father's plot or trade and the rest of the sons were supposed to apprentice themselves to others of mostly similar trade. This was true across urban and rural settings and forced the bulk of migratory activities.

As is similar to the apprenticeships that we see today, there was typically a long decade of servitude to the master followed by an independent practice of trade, either in the same city or in a different one which would take another decade to firmly establish.

Hence, people were more or less locked on to their trades at the beginning of their apprenticeship. Women's participation in the workforce was primarily as extra limbs for agriculture or as unpaid labor in the many small family businesses; independence in terms of career was an alien concept as such.

Though the Indian Civil Services opened up their doors to Indians only in 1864, it took almost till independence for any meaningful participation of the workforce in the Government sector to happen. Socialist India adopted the Soviet model of industrialization and established Larger Public Sector undertakings which helped households to manage their basic requirements of food, clothing, and shelter.

Both my parents grew up in large lower middle- class families which were characterized by a few hands that earned, and many more mouths that needed to be fed. If a fresh entrant to the workforce

Before We Begin...

found himself (and very rarely herself) with a government job, he clung on to it for dear life and adjusted the arrangements of the household around whatever income his salary paid.

The value proposition of an employer was as a provider of a place to work, a salary at the end of the month, and an assured pension at the end of a forty-year tenure.

Commentaries around careers in the two decades starting from 1970 are best represented by the Angry Young Man image that trended across different languages of Indian cinema.

So many people, so few jobs!

This was also broadly the reason that the now cliched preference of Indian parents for the choice of their children's careers to be either medicine, engineering or the law started getting entrenched. By natural extension, the brain drain of such trained professionals to countries like the US and the UK also started at the same time. There were high barriers to entry for aspirants to any other non-conventional careers.

From the 1990s onwards, as we opened up our sectors to private participation, the real explosion of organized jobs in the Private Sector began. As our appetites for risk increased aided by factors like access to capital, democratization of knowledge, and most importantly the accumulation of wealth of our parent's generations, we Indians have started to rethink careers.

A corollary to this fact is the burgeoning number of private coaching classes for competitive exams which have mushroomed since this time. We also witnessed the professionalization of many

Indian private firms as they started getting exposed to global business practices and the need for trained professionals grew.

Indians also learned about how professionals around the world, especially the Westerners have managed their own careers. Female participation in the Industries and Services sector has started picking up.

The last decade or so has truly been revolutionary for the workplace in India. India does not have enough Companies in the Organized, Corporate sector to fully cover the employment needs of its trained youth, and this, if anything, is the single most important reason that we require entrepreneurship.

Our long track record of being a country which is a continuously growing economy, a stable polity, and a people with a large number of English speakers help us attract capital from all over the world like few other countries can.

It is now not unusual for even undergraduates with little family money to confidently embark on their own business projects with the inherent confidence of success as well as the fact that the downsides of failure can be mitigated.

Young, mid-career, and older professionals switch between employment and entrepreneurship and are valued for both these career paths. In this context, careers are more fluid than ever before. In a job, just growth in terms of regular metrics like position, designation, and salaries/perks is necessary but not sufficient. Employees need a work environment where they can thrive a greater sense of responsibility and acknowledgment that their work is adding value to the firm.

Before We Begin...

These 4 distinct stages where people's paradigms about careers have changed, primarily demonstrated by the increase in risk-taking ability are tabulated below for your reference.

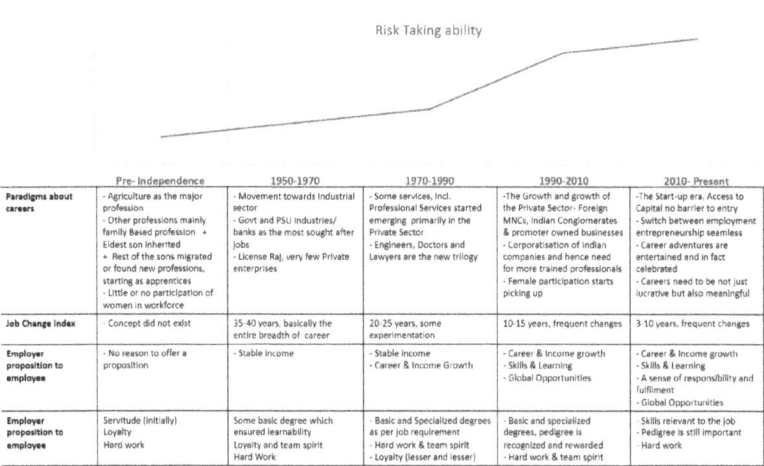

	Pre- Independence	1950-1970	1970-1990	1990-2010	2010- Present
Paradigms about careers	- Agriculture as the major profession - Other professions mainly family Based profession +Eldest son inherited + Rest of the sons migrated or found new professions, starting as apprentices - Little or no participation of women in workforce	- Movement towards Industrial sector - Govt and PSU Industries/ banks as the most sought after jobs - License Raj, very few Private enterprises	- Some services, Incl. Professional Services started emerging primarily in the Private Sector - Engineers, Doctors and Lawyers are the new trilogy	-The Growth and growth of the Private Sector,- Foreign MNCs, Indian Conglomerates & promoter owned businesses - Corporatisation of Indian companies and hence need for more trained professionals - Female participation starts picking up	-The Start-up era. Access to Capital no barrier to entry - Switch between employment entrepreneurship seamless - Career adventures are entertained and in fact celebrated - Careers need to be not just lucrative but also meaningful
Job Change Index	- Concept did not exist	35-40 years, basically the entire breadth of career	20-25 years, some experimentation	10-15 years, frequent changes	3-10 years, frequent changes
Employer proposition to employee	- No reason to offer a proposition	- Stable Income	- Stable Income - Career & Income Growth	- Career & Income growth - Skills & Learning - Global Opportunities	- Career & Income growth - Skills & Learning - A sense of responsibility and fulfilment - Global Opportunities
Employer proposition to employee	Servitude (Initially) Loyalty Hard work	Some basic degree which ensured learnability Loyalty and team spirit Hard Work	- Basic and Specialized degrees as per job requirement - Hard work & team spirit - Loyalty (lesser and lesser)	- Basic and specialized degrees, pedigree is recognized and rewarded - Hard work & team spirit	- Skills relevant to the job - Pedigree is still important - Hard work

Going further, I want to highlight two undercurrents that will impact us and would like the reader to always consider.

The first undercurrent is the dynamics of supply-demand in the workforce and the additional qualification of available workforce which is trained and skilled for jobs. Consider IT salaries as a case in point. The below chart from <u>Business Today</u> shows how fresher salaries have more or less stagnated over the past decade whereas CEO salaries have leapfrogged.

What do we make out of this ? Is there zero value to the skill that a fresher starts off with ? Is the influx of aspirants to the IT sector overwhelmingly large that this is driving the salary market into a negative auction of sorts ?

	(₹ Crore)		(₹ Lakh)	
	2022	2012	2022	2012
TCS	26	8	4	1.6
Infosys	79	0.8	3.6	2.75
Wipro	79	5.1	3.5	2.4
HCL	124	8.4	3.5	3
Tech Mahindra	63	1	3.4	2.5
Average Salary	74.2	4.66	3.6	2.45
Median Salary	79	5.1	3.5	2.5
Increase in 10 years	1449 %		40%	

Business Today, Dec 2022

Then, there is the dreaded "Mid-life crisis". The definition of this crisis itself is volatile, for I am not sure anymore when this is supposed to start; at age 45, 35, or even 25 ? Somehow I feel that most people around me are not completely happy with their career path and their present status and always want to do something else. To check this, ask 10 random friends and acquaintances and you will be convinced that I am not far from the truth.

Career fulfillment is elusive. Got a high salary with a great role ? The hours are long. Or the commute is a disaster. Maybe all the above can be dealt with, but the boss is another story altogether. The list goes on and on.

I feel this sense of being in crisis mode is a combination of three factors; a sense of non- autonomy over time, non- achievement of financial independence, and carrying sunk costs (in other words, regret) over choices made and paths traveled. A combination of even two of these can make people age, and appear to age much faster than even bad dietary or exercise habits.

It is a paradox that we live in perhaps the times of greatest peace that the world has ever seen in its entire history but that still does not guarantee that we are happier than people of earlier decades and centuries. Our work plays a key role in contributing to this paradox.

Funnily enough, I feel that this is a scenario where the older learn from the younger. As Millenials and their later generations start to emphasize more on careers of choice based on purpose, personal growth and development, and work-life balance, the earlier generations which are still in the workforce will also start to re-examine their career paths.

Can we try to be better equipped to enter the workforce ? Can we develop a better sense of how our work and career should span out and actively seek options that let us pursue them ? I believe that my book will help many of the readers through some of these questions. We owe it to ourselves to have fulfilling careers and consequently fulfilling lives like Sir MV had, if not as long as his life and work spanned.

THE PURPOSE OF THIS BOOK AND ITS INTENDED AUDIENCE

𝓟ersonal disclosure. Different from the case of many writers in this genre of Self-Help books, my own life story is no inspiration to others as my own career cannot be termed as successful enough or even a lighthouse of clarity. I have meandered along different paths both in reality and definitely a thousand times more in my headspace.

I have had some very broad ideas about what I have wanted to study and work on and have generally followed it but the exact path I have taken makes sense, and that too only in retrospect to exactly one individual; me.

The Purpose of this Book and its Intended Audience

Has this lack of a crystal clear career roadmap, and an appropriate action plan followed by actions affected whatever I believe is my career success? maybe a little bit and again it depends on whom you ask. Me, my parents, my wife, my friends and colleagues, or maybe my child in the future.

The insights I derive are partly from my own experiences and predominantly from my experience of close to 6 years of interaction with around 500 + students and professionals with whom I have discussed and mentored on either offers or admits.

There have been people whom I know intimately but a far greater number of these 500 have cold-called me through Linkedin or through a wonderful firm I work with, Gocrackit. Why have so many people approached me? It is mostly the amalgamation of some biases on their part.

- **Proximity & Availability**- for people who are directly acquainted with me.
- **Halo Effect**- because I got admitted to College A, I must also be able to help people get admitted to College B which has a similar admissions procedure.
- **Recency**: Being an alumnus or an ex-employee, my opinion about that college or firm should be very close to the facts.

Whether or not I have been of help to these friends and acquaintances, the experience has been enriching for me as I've been able to learn about multiple personalities, companies, and industries without having to spend much except my own time.

I have had the good sense to be a prodigious note-taker since a very young age and hence have compiled copious amounts of material on this topic which when synthesized coherently seems deserving of a book by itself. And surely, there are enough common threads and patterns available for a decent synthesis.

It was probably in May 2022 that I began to actively entertain the thought that this book might indeed be a good idea. That month was interesting because, in a span of a week or so, I had conversations regarding career choices with people in every decade of different age groups of the eligible workforce, from people in their 20s to those in their 60s.

And one thing that struck me crystal clear, is that very few people have any absolute clarity about where their career aspirations lie.

We have more vivid and concrete opinions about less relevant things like politics, religion, sports teams, cuisines, and so on! The lack of clarity is ubiquitous and requires urgent attention.

By virtue of reading quite a few self-help books on my Kindle Oasis, I get automatic recommendations on a lot of books in this genre. In all these years of using the Kindle Store, I am yet to get a recommendation on books that help people crack admits and offers. For the past few months, I made a further targeted search of books on the same and still did not come up with anything close.

Why focus on Admits and Offers? Simply put, College Admits and Job offers are the two biggest launchpads of any contemporary, 21st Century Professional Career. While one gets to seek and receive college admits in two or three dispersed timeframes, the same is spread across perhaps a dozen or so in the case of job offers.

The Purpose of this Book and its Intended Audience

These timeframes are a bundle of emotions all rolled into one. The hope of a better future, the agony of waiting, the high of a successful admission/ offer, and the low of a dream not converted.

It helps to have a sextant and a compass for positioning and navigation and my fervent hope is that this book plays both these roles.

The readership that I have written this book for ranges from students who are on the cusp of completing their undergraduate studies to mid-career professionals up to the age of 40 or so. I have not had experiences beyond this age range and hence have restrained from commenting much about choices regarding undergraduate studies or careers of 40+-year-olds.

At the Postgraduate level, I am most comfortable discussing STEM- based Master's courses and MBA options as I have a Master's Degree in Engineering and an MBA. I would believe that what I have to say here would not be tangentially different in the case of any generic postgraduate course.

Does this book help you become a pilot, a cricketer, or say a soldier ? Not really, for the entry criteria differ drastically for these career options as compared to working in a corporate job. However, some aspects covered in this book like understanding how to present oneself in the written form or how to empathize better with an interview panel and hence prepare yourself are universally applicable and hence could be of some value.

Another thing that strikes me about admits and offers as topics is that they fall so squarely inside the radar of every individual's self-interest that not a great deal of motivation is required to get the undivided attention of people. In a sense, they are similar to topics like personal finance or fitness.

And, comparable to these topics, there is absolutely no way that any strict or narrow maxims could apply to the general populace.

Keeping this in mind, here are a few pointers on how I interpret this book and its success and also expect you, my reader, to do so:

- This book is not about facts but purely based on my point of view. It helps that there is no standard or certifying body on career management either locally or globally which lays out strictures on what can and cannot be preached.
- What I am attempting to compile here are talking points and broad frameworks that could be used when seeking help and preparing for both admits and offers.
- I would consider this book to be immensely successful if it helps you reduce your time for preparation without reducing its effectiveness.
- The ideal way to seek advice is to be very specific in the ask and factor out the inherent biases of people giving the advice. I hope this book helps you on both accounts.
- Even after multiple people have given you advice, you are okay with conflicting points of view and go along with what you seem is the most actionable and relevant.
- You can use the book to prepare career plans along different parameters and measure yourself against these plans at the right intervals. Doing this gives you the confidence to avoid comparing yourself against others as there is no benefit to this exercise.

The Purpose of this Book and its Intended Audience

- Like in many books, you may find the whole book useful or only specific parts of it.
- Ultimately, you are able to live in peace with the decision that has been taken by concluding that whatever best could be done has been done. If my book helps you to minimize regret over your career, I would consider it to be wildly successful.

THE BLUEPRINT OF THIS BOOK

*H*ow should this book be used ? I hope it makes sense to you to either read it as a whole or pick up and use certain chapters as is required for a situation; the pursuit of either an admit or an offer.

Since most of us crave structure; here is the simplified structure of this book

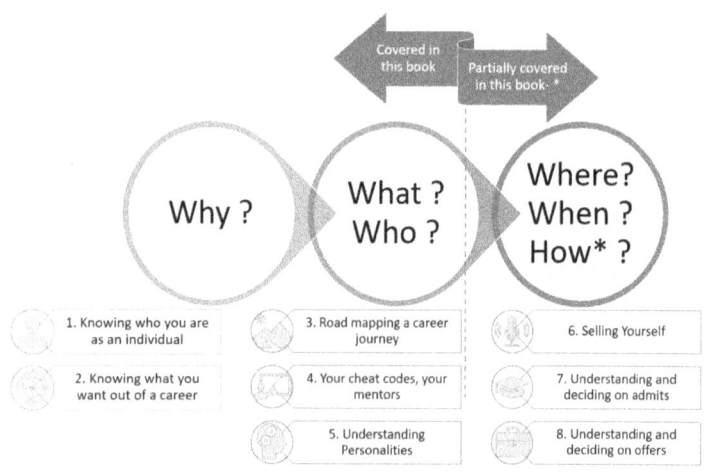

The Blueprint of this Book

To borrow from the phrase popularized by Simon Sinek through his book and videos, we start with why. Though the word purpose has very broad connotations, it is used in the context of this book to understand you through two lenses; who you are as an individual and what you want out of your career.

The broad plan to achieve your career goals is discussed in the section on road mapping. Subsequently, the key personalities involved are mentioned with a highlight on mentors and using their help effectively.

The last section is focused on helping you sell yourself to the above personalities through different media like resumes, cover letters, and application essays. Finally, we take a look at the approach to be pursued when presented with one or more admit or offer and at the way to make reasonable and optimal decisions.

KNOWING YOURSELF

> *"If you know the enemy and know yourself, you need not fear the result of a hundred battles. If you know yourself but not the enemy, for every victory gained you will also suffer a defeat. If you know neither the enemy nor yourself, you will succumb in every battle."*
>
> **– Sun Tzu, The Art of War**

While the intent of this book is not to prepare anyone to go to war, the takeaway from this famous Art of War quote is that knowing yourself is an immensely important, and often underestimated endeavor. While most of us view ourselves as the heroes and heroines of our own stories, we often do not have a clear storyline in place or adhere to one if it exists. There is seldom any attempt to match an individual's interest to available options.

In fact, I have hardly heard of any career counseling conducted in India during the formative years of one's youth. Careers are usually zeroed in based on family lineage (my mother is a lawyer), safety in terms of predictable incomes (doctors or engineers), or some visually discernible (but low bandwidth) traits.

Every individual is such an incredible mosaic of aspirations, talents, traits, experiences, and backgrounds. It seems like a herculean task for even a trained mind to catalog and analyze all this information into actionable intelligence. However, even a small portion of time spent on reflection is bound to reap rich dividends.

Reflection on self- identity is absolutely critical from the perspective of careers. Irrespective of what we set out to do, we need to have the passion and the commitment to stick on for reasonably long periods of time. A lack of self- identity and purpose makes it harder to cross hurdles of which there are bound to be plenty in a long career.

Two aspects. Knowing who you are and knowing what you want.

When mapped in fairly elaborate detail using simple tools outlined below, this provides a workable and satisfactory North star when planning for careers.

Knowing who you are

> "There are three extremely hard things: steel, a diamond, and to know one's self."
>
> – Benjamin Franklin

There is good news to make this hard thing of knowing one's self easier; a kind of fast food version, if you may. They are called Psychometric tests. They help to understand what your skills, interests, preferences, and values are. There are many tests that you could undertake yourself whereas others may require guidance.

These tests will not accurately identify the right course or job for you. Rather, they help you in understanding yourself and articulating your preferences. This, in turn, allows you to compare them with other available options.

Some tests will help you choose an area of specialization to study, while others might help you to hone a particular style of communication. Some of them could help you during negotiations and resolving conflicts. The broad categorization of what these tests bring out are as follows:-

- Personality types: These are a combination of social and professional drives, needs, and attitudes. Your personality type largely determines whether you're suitable for a certain type of work or working environment. A popular example is the Myers-Briggs Type Indicator (MBTI) assessment tool. This tool might be the most relevant to our discussion here and will be explained in detail elsewhere.

- Interests: The theory here is that your interests determine what you like doing most, as has also been demonstrated by psychological studies. The Strong Interest Inventory takes someone's interests as a strong indicator for a particular career path. These interests are of six types: realistic, artistic, investigative, social, enterprising, and conventional. This is mapped against different areas like risk- taking, learning environment, and so on.
- Values at work: Autonomy, work-life balance, responsibility, and so on are values that can be culled out from employees and used to determine fit in a given role or even for the company itself in the case of aspiring candidates.
- Abilities: There is a section in this book devoted to standardized tests so more on this later. Common abilities that are tested are mental aptitude, reading comprehension, verbal ability in a relevant language, and so on.

Popular self-assessment tools

Myers- Brigg Type Indicator Test:

As explained succinctly in Wikipedia, this test is based on Carl Jung's theory of psychological types which states that people experience the world using four primary psychological functions, one of which is dominant in any individual most of the time:-

- Introversion/ Extraversion
- Intuition/ Sensing
- Feeling/ Thinking
- Judging/ Perceiving.

The combination of two options each from these 4 categories results in 16 unique types of personalities. These types determine how these people express themselves, analyze data, and make decisions. Jung has classified these personality types into,

- Analysts- Architects, military commanders, and debaters. Logical think ers who need to plan for everything, display an enormous appetite for knowledge and love intellectual challenges.
- Diplomats- Advocates, arbitrators, co-ordinators and campaigners. Quiet types who prefer to take a backstage role, know how to inspire their co-workers, enthusiastic and creative, and are relentless idealists.
- Sentinels- Logisticians, management executives, consuls. Practical, dedicated, reliable people who are skilled at managing others.
- Explorers- Adventurers, entrepreneurs, entertainers. Exhibit charm, spontaneity, and flexibility and are ready to try new things.

DISC Assessment:

This is used to predict job performance using workstyle preferences and habits. The test uses 4 dimensions to group personality type:

1. Dominance – Emphasis on producing results along with confidence
2. Influence – Relationship building and persuasion
3. Steadiness – Dependability, sincerity, co operation
4. Conscientiousness – quality and accuracy as related to expertise and competency

Big Five Assessment

The Big Five personality theory assigns a score based on the following five personality traits:

- Extraversion – outgoing/energetic vs. solitary/reserved
- Agreeableness – friendly/compassionate vs. challenging/callous
- Neuroticism – sensitive/nervous vs. resilient/confident
- Conscientiousness – efficient/organized vs. extravagant/careless
- Openness to experience – inventive/curious vs. consistent/cautious

Knowing what you want

Many of us dive into careers with the intention to earn a livelihood through money, to gain standing in our society, to become famous, or even to explore new experiences. The compulsion of any one or more of the above factors often overpowers any systematic approach we may have attempted to planning our careers.

And, this continues well into the first, second, third, and fourth decades of our careers. With every turn and twist of the road, only the characters, the circumstances, the conversations, and the choices change.

The environment is also not enabling, either. In the past 16 years or so since I graduated from College, we have witnessed multiple economic shocks that put many a plan into jeopardy. It is hard to predict the short term accurately and harder to even think about the longer term, let's say 5 years from now. When the outward is so volatile, we have no choice but to look inward.

I feel that we should plan, roughly every 3 years or so, to pause and reflect on what we want out of our careers. It is always my claim that even if we do not know what we want to do, knowing what we do not want to do is a good enough place to start and we can build further on the same.

What should a reflection of the self with an intent to make career choices include ? In my own opinion, it should be the following:-

1. Doing what makes me happy ?
2. Doing what comes naturally to me ?
3. Doing what gives me a sense of fulfillment and responsibility ?
4. Doing what paves the path to career progression ?

5. Doing what makes me prosperous ?
6. Doing what utilizes to the best extent my prior background/ education training ?
7. Doing what gives me the resources to be the most complete person I can be, even outside of work ?

Let me use a few pages to elaborate on each of the above. You may add to the list if you feel that you want to articulate and track another aspect not mentioned above.

Doing what makes me happy

While there are many ways in which to define happiness, my intuitive interpretation of it leans towards a state of pleasantness, lightness, being aware, and being in control. By means of corollary, one could also think of situations where one is not unhappy.

Choosing work that makes us happy is necessary but not a sufficient condition to make our overall lives happier. It also makes us perform optimally at work as it is often a prerequisite for achieving flow, a state in which our creativity, mental health, and productivity are enhanced.

Happiness at work can be interpreted along multiple dimensions. The kind of ambiance , the nature of the role and responsibilities, the kind of people engaged with, the adrenaline rush of doing something new all the time or the certainty of a stable salary, working hours, and expectations. Define your version of happiness.

Doing what comes naturally to me

When I started playing cricket, left arm off spin came naturally to me. I had, on various occasions tried to keep wickets but somehow the work behind the stumps always seemed to be an onerous one. Whereas it is true that with hard work, we can mitigate many of our limitations, it is often wiser, faster, and more economical to pick up the skill that we know we are good at and build on it to a level where we are unbeatable.

In this regard, consider the popular 10000 hours rule, which says that you only achieve expertise if you practice something for said hours. Would you rather spend the whole of this time doing something that comes naturally to you or something you struggle with even after the first 1000 hours or so ?

Are you good with numbers ? Are you able to convince people around your point of view ? Are you able to negotiate complex contracts effectively ? Every one of these skills has its own place.

It is easier to develop stamina into doing what you do naturally. Do anything else and you will be swimming against the tide. I believe that we need to have a minimum threshold of ability across a variety of skill levels and then focus on improving strengths to optimize in our chosen fields.

Doing what gives me a sense of fulfillment and responsibility

I once had a College Professor explain that Corporate jobs are more lucrative than academic ones because they are more boring. As I go longer and longer into my corporate career, I begin to appreciate this sentiment better.

Many, many corporate jobs, especially in middle management pay you for being available for any situation and being responsible for outcomes, processes, and people. Much of your effective working hours is spent on things that you would not have, as a young kid imagined you would end up doing. Meetings, reviews, waiting for information, and preparing reports. In this humdrum, you need to find a larger purpose at work or the days will seem interminably long.

For much of my career, it has been to make a factory ready for production within a stipulated time and recently, to make sure our customers have the vehicle they need when they come looking. All of the above mundane activities are incidental, to be navigated through to get to the purpose. I am pretty sure my purpose at work will keep changing often. It is natural and part of a growth process. Every one of us needs to find this purpose which will keep us fulfilled and give us a sense of responsibility.

Many a path may not be very lucrative but can be fulfilling. Teaching in India is not a vocation that often sees commensurate pay, but I'm yet to come across a teacher who regardless doesn't have a twinkle in her eye when being part of the kid's learning journey.

I stay next to the Art of Living Ashram in Bengaluru and I can imagine that many of the people who work here full- time can find regular, higher- paying jobs but they choose to volunteer for a purpose which best fills their time. The sense of purpose is often enough to overcome the lack of the many material comforts that money offers.

Doing what paves the path to career progression

You know the cliched interview question, "Where do you see yourself 5 years from now ?" There are a lot of career options where one can take a cursory glance at websites like LinkedIn, Glassdoor, or Indeed and figure out the rungs of the ladder. Oftentimes, there is a predictable (though obviously rigorous) path to success in many of these fields but we can also sometimes not even have an idea.

I know of many firms which place a premium on loyalty to the company as manifested through the number of years of service in the same company. Some others, which anyway experience high attrition would perhaps favor fresh blood with experience from outside. Other firms want expertise from outside. Many, many senior jobs in public policy, sales and business development, and professional services like law and chartered accountancy are available to you because of your network. Leading large teams and businesses across different roles is one path, establishing world- class expertise in a narrow field is another.

Career progression is not just about higher salaries, bigger offices, better perks, or more fame. It is also about being entrusted with more responsibilities, taking up more challenging work, and having greater skin in the game. All of these are major motivating factors to ensure that we do not lose our passion for the job.

Doing what makes me prosperous

Do you earn enough to spend, save & invest, and then have a bit more disposable income ? Can this process be increased linearly, if not exponentially ? Do you have a long gestation period before you start earning money (like in becoming a doctor), or is it relatively shorter but maybe less lucrative (like in the humanities)?

I know of this individual who was in the entertainment industry. Because he was starring in a lead role for a particular TV series, he was contractually obligated to not sign up for any other production house. And, his payment was on a daily basis whenever shoots involving him used to happen. Though this job made him famous, it was financially unsustainable as the number of shoots per month for him used to vary based on the plot. He left very soon to pursue a stable job in a completely new area.

Is your career option extremely well (albeit narrowly) defined like in government services where the reward is the position and not necessarily the money that comes with it ? Consider all of these very well.

Doing what utilizes to the best extent my prior background/ education training

College education is very expensive, both in terms of time and money. Still, many of us end up pursuing one and then doing something totally unconnected. Similar to work experience gained, especially in the initial 3- 5 years of our careers.

When viewed through the lens of sunk cost, we should only focus forward to our next endeavor. However, we gain an advantage by performing jobs that utilize our earlier work experience or education because of the familiarity, the practice, or the tacit understanding that we carry with us.

There are added benefits, like the continuity of a network of classmates and colleagues who forge ahead on the same path and are available for any support. A few years ago, I had a choice to join either a startup in the same industry I was working in or the World's largest company by market cap (as of October 2023). I chose the former and my dad went bonkers over this decision !

My rationale, however, was that I was working in an industry and in a product segment that held the promise of explosive growth, and hence it made sense for me to continue in the same industry rather than to go work for that behemoth.

That being said, there is a great merit in exploring the unknown and the uncertain. My opinion is that we should consider industry and role as two dimensions and explore new things one dimension at a time. Say, in my case, from automotive manufacturing to medical devices manufacturing or from automotive manufacturing to automotive sales.

Doing what gives me the resources to be the most complete person I can be, even outside of work

Beyond all of the above, let us not forget that our work and career are parts of our life, not our entire life itself. The weightage that we give to them may vary based on our predispositions.

My take on work- life balance is that both work and life need to reinforce each other, albeit in their own ways. Imagine them as providing different sorts of energies. Work, through the money to spend, the places to visit, and the things to learn. Life, through the memories of time spent with family and friends, the people you help, and a myriad other things. It is very hard to be at peace when one pulls down the other. Inevitably, both will collapse.

Frameworks

So, what does it all add up to ? A mosaic of who you are and what you want, to be used as a backdrop against any opportunities you are pursuing. The correlation is not mathematical, and it will be often difficult to evaluate two similar opportunities. However, there will be a glaring difference between what you believe you can and should be pursuing and what you shouldn't, saving you loads of time and effort.

The best way to keep a running tab of the same is to fill up a table like the one below, which you keep tracking in the present and see how it has changed in retrospect. 2 to 3 years is a good timeframe in my opinion, and if too many things do not change across the columns, it gives you an insight on your personality and how it is evolving. I have used the MBTI test framework as an example,

	2017	2020	2023
Introversion/ Extraversion			
Intuition/ Sensing			
Feeling/ Thinking			
Judging/ Perceiving.			
Doing what makes me happy			
Doing what comes naturally to me			
Doing what gives me the sense of fulfillment and responsibility			
Doing what paves the path to career progression			
Doing what makes me prosperous			
Doing what utilizes to the best extent my prior background/ education training			
Doing what gives me the resources to be the most complete person I can be, even outside of work ?			

YOUR CHEAT CODES, YOUR MENTORS

> "Mentoring is a brain to pick, an ear to listen, and a push in the right direction."
>
> – **John C. Crosby,**
> *Former US Representative*

Among the very few things that I have absolutely done right in my career is to have stints where my reporting managers have always been at least a decade older than me. Initially, this was inadvertent but very quickly, I realized the value of this maxim and have clung on to it for dear life.

The implicit qualification in this statement has been that every one of these bosses has been personally invested in my success and provided me with the canvas that it takes to do so. I am an outlier in this regard as many of these former bosses are people I still turn to for advice and are hence valued mentors. I don't think everyone is so lucky and I also don't take my good fortune for granted.

It is great to have brilliant and supportive colleagues but seeking and getting mentorship is the path to magical careers. Often, we get lost in the humdrum of our work and forget to seek advice from Let me qualify what according to me are the attributes of a great mentor and how one should utilize that mentor's time.

Choosing a mentor

- Almost always, the mentor is at least 5 years older than you. Somebody who has a lesser age difference is likely to give very tactical advice which might be only marginally useful. She or he might have a point of view suitable for application in a very specific circumstance but not otherwise. You might also run into the off chance that he or she considers you to be a competition and might foster some kind of malice which would result in ill-meaning advice.
- Family members can often be very good mentors. They know you like none other. However, use the first point here religiously.
- The mentor should be from a similar firm, industry, role, or any combination of the above. If the mentor additionally has a varied experience on any of these parameters, this advice is even more useful as his/her peripheral vision is only heightened.
- Teachers are generally interested in the welfare of their former students. Many of them might seem to be aloof when you

are on campus, but I have always found them to be more approachable when you become an alumnus.
- How many mentors should you have? Between 3 to 5, in my opinion. Consider them as the Board of Directors of the Company which is you, the Individual. In the same way that Companies strive for diversity in their Board, you should have diverse mentors whom you know will have varying world views. Additionally, remember that you are still the Chairman/Chairwoman of this Board.

Engaging with a mentor

- You are able to discuss the Whys of a problem or a situation with your mentor, not just the Hows, Whats, Wheres, and Whens.
- Both you and the mentor are brutally honest with each other.
- The mentor should necessarily know you beyond your workplace as this helps the mentor consider perspectives similarly as you do. It is up to you to provide the mentor with this license by engaging with him/her beyond work and work-based transactions.
- It does not matter to the mentor if you have previously gone along with his/her advice or not. The mentor understands and appreciates that his/her advice is just one more point of view, though an important one.
- The mentor usually doesn't offer unsolicited advice except in circumstances where you are bordering on the insane, unethical, criminal, or career-destroying in your behavior .
- Utilize a work-based mentor for academic-based advice and vice versa. Their opinions will be refreshingly different.

- You should ideally discuss with the mentor to
  - Frame structures and processes to solve near to medium term work-based problems.
  - Compare and contrast admits and offers, especially when deciding how to evaluate similar choices.
  - Seek an introduction to a firm or an individual that you are keen on interacting with.
  - Use mentors less than 5 years older than you, who are almost your contemporaries for preparation for admits or offers like mock interviews, resume reviews, essays, and so on. Unless they do this routinely.
- You should definitely not discuss with the mentor about
  - Individuals at work or school that you have a problem with. There is little to zero chance that they could or would do anything about it.
  - Gossip about mutual acquaintances. This is a sure-shot way of losing the intrinsic trust and respect built into this relationship. If so tempted to gossip, use your friends, family, or partners instead.
  - Seeking help to influence decisions surrounding admits or offers.
  - Getting into business or money-based transactions.

ROADMAPPING A CAREER JOURNEY

> *In preparing for battle I have always found that plans are useless but planning is indispensable.*
>
> **– Dwight Eisenhower**

In keeping with the spirit of the above quote, while the verbatim of the roadmap itself might be of varying degrees of usefulness, it is the process of articulation of thoughts into paper that benefits the most.

Writing inevitably leads to Systems 2 thinking, a slow, deliberate, and logical way of thought. (for more on this, read Daniel Kahneman's 2011 book, *Thinking, Fast and Slow*). I had written a blog on the benefits of writing in <u>Medium</u> and as per my hierarchy of preference of learning tools,

Mind mapping >> Hand writing > Writing on a device > Typing on a device >> Reading

Mind maps are even better and I will try to incorporate as many of these as they help to frame better perspectives. I would recommend them to you in whatever form or shape you deem best.

A roadmap can be completely private and to be shared with only the closest of mentors and confidants, only if deemed essential. I state this for two reasons,

a. No one except you is going to take responsibility for these roadmaps anyway.
b. The contents of the roadmap and the way they change are going to make complete sense only to you.

I advocate that every individual map should contain three different career parameters along with different timelines; roles, money, and skills. These three should ideally be placed one on top of the other and my preference of order is roles/ designations, money, and skills.

Some pointers on how to do effective roadmaps without boiling the ocean.

- Time frame and Least Count of roadmaps
    - Role/ Designation:- 3 to 5 years time frame with a Least count of 0.5 or 1 year.
    - Money/ Salary:- 3 to 5 years time frame with a Least count of 0.5 or 1 year.
    - Skills:- 1 year to 5 years.

Anything beyond 5 years is not going to be of much use in the context of VUCA (Volatility, Uncertainty, Chaos & Ambiguity) and BANI (Brittle, Anxious, Non-linear & Incomprehensible). The farther out in time, the lesser will be the accuracy of the forecast.

- Crowdsourcing information from people you are already acquainted with and who are non-competitive is the best way to start. LinkedIn and Glassdoor are the next best bets.
- The aim is to be accurate and not precise, it should not have less than 5 data points and more than 10 data points. We are not conducting critical medical trials here.
- When benchmarking, look at the relevance of data. Geography, degrees, company, etc..
- Benchmark only during the preparation of roadmaps and not otherwise. How others perform in their career usually has zero causation with how you will do in yours.

Consider the illustration of this triad of roadmaps for a person with around 8 years of experience, working currently as a Deputy Manager in Manufacturing Operations in the Automotive sector. It is an easier task than usual because the career and money progressions are usually well-regimented and transparent for the entire organization to understand. In-house talent rises through the ranks and high-potential individuals traverse the same path, albeit at a steeper pace.

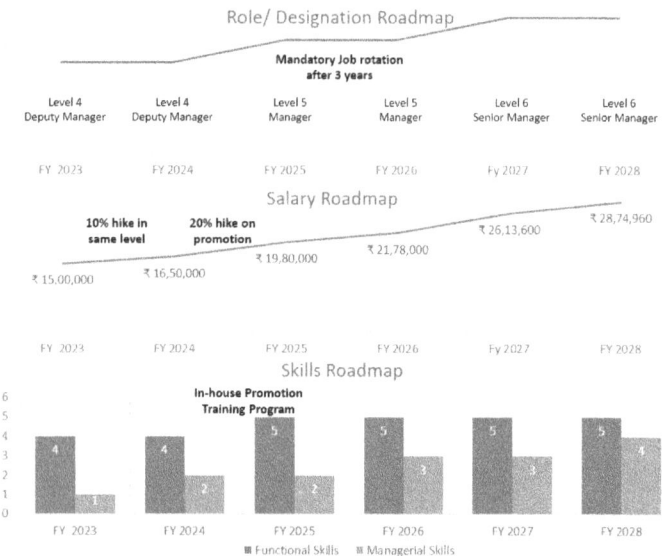

The above is a straightforward roadmap. Add to it the following twists and turns

- What job rotations offer the best learning and development ?
- What skills do I need ? Are they better obtained inside the firm or outside ?
- Is it worthwhile to take a break and go to Graduate school either for a Master's Degree or an MBA ? Should it be a sabbatical or a clean exit from the firm followed by an attempt at placements a year later? How have students who had the same incoming profile fared after graduation? Full time or Part time/ weekend ? the best chance of progression?
- Does it make sense to change firms? If so, same industry and role, or different? More on this in the subsequent section.
- Do I anticipate or desire a greater amount of money ? If so, what is the best way to gain more, and how best to negotiate ?

Among the three roadmaps, the one on roles requires more elaboration. If done rightly, Skills and salaries will naturally follow.

Role/ Designation Roadmapping

The role/ designation levels are well documented and should very easily be available all the way up to the highest designation in the Company. There are often paths of progression which lead to

- Specialization & hence expertise or general management & hence greater responsibilities.
- Corporate or planning-based roles, or Operational or execution-based roles.

It is my fervent belief that the major part of midlife crises that professionals encounter in the workplace is that though they recognize the above paths, they are pretty much confused about what to do next. Status quo or change? If change, is it Company/ Industry or role? Also, there is a lot of comparison with peers of similar age and qualification in terms of career progress.

Writing this down in the ambit of any framework is the start of getting more clarity. While the choice of specialization or general management can be thought of as a medium to long-term selection , I feel that it is better to switch from planning to execution-based roles within a period of around 3 years.

Leading from earlier points, the duo of parameters to be often considered simultaneously is industry-role. Below is a framework which I have found to be the most useful. Let us continue with the example of someone working in Automotive manufacturing.

Admits and Offers

Over a period of time, this 2x2 matrix can be used to fill up movement in terms of roles for an individual.

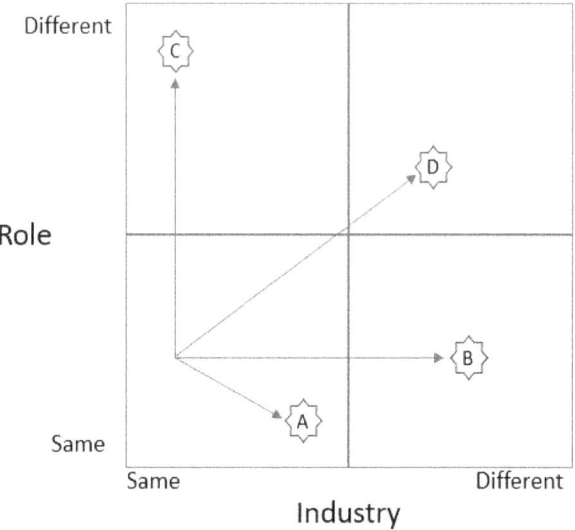

- A- Remaining in Automotive manufacturing. This might mean changing the firm for the same role in another automotive OEM or working in another plant/ location. This is usually the easiest in terms of effort needed to change over. It might or might not be the most lucrative though.

- B- Shifting from Automotive manufacturing to say, aerospace manufacturing. The functional skills required are the same, only a little bit of re-orientation might be required. For example, automotive manufacturing might require more focus on cost and unit economics. whereas, aerospace manufacturing would require a disproportionate focus on quality and first- time right. This necessarily means changing the company unless you work for a conglomerate and such opportunities crop up within.

C- Shifting from Automotive manufacturing to say, automotive sales. The industry cycles are the same and hence the nuances/tacit knowledge but the nature of the work might vary. It is often advisable to do this within a firm because of familiarity with the Company's ways of working as well as with the people involved. Both B & C are medium hard in terms of effort required.

D- Shifting from Automotive manufacturing to say, IT sales. This is the most difficult transition and often requires huge intervention like another degree, an advanced certification or an extreme like starting on your own as previous work experience is not very relevant.

Making your roadmap that extra notch effective

- Understand the most important cognitive biases that come into play. Some examples are:-

a. Sunk Cost- Are you worrying about decisions that have already been taken ?
b. Opportunity cost- Are you evaluating a particular decision alongside every other opportunity that is mutually exclusive to this ?
c. Anchoring- Are you willing to look at new facts and opinions and change your own mind or opinion if so required ?
d. Availability- Are you going ahead with an option just because it's easily available
e. Confirmation- Are you taking inputs from only places and sources that only confirm what you already believe ?
f. Cognitive dissonance- Are you shutting out the likelihood of disastrous negative events from happening ?
g. Halo effect- Just because you are good at one thing, do you automatically assume that you are good at another ?

The list is endless. To understand these better, I recommend Daniel Kahnemann's works.

- In each of the momentous career decisions you have to make, lay down what success looks like. Nowadays, this is so easy with LinkedI n, Indeed, Glassdoor, and the like . This forms the basis of your plan to understand and approach the person who would be most pertinent to give you career advice at any given point in time. Additional qualification, not someone who has decades more experience than you but ideally someone 4 to 5 years older.

- At any given point in time, think mostly about having stretch goals, which are a little beyond reasonable, and a couple of fantasy goals which are beyond the realm of possibility. The stretch goals give you confidence to keep going in the long haul, as you keep ticking them off your to-do list and the fantasy goals keep you in the game for many long years.
- Use different sources like interviews, biographies, and even fiction to understand what goes into the day in the life of the person carrying out the role. This is critical to see if you can imagine yourself doing that job day in and day out throughout your career. For example, John Grisham's novels provide a great insight into how lawyers work.
- Internships are a low- cost, no- failure option to find out what careers interest you and suit you. Especially when changing careers or taking a break to go to college, please be very cognizant of using this option to the fullest extent.
- Review your roadmaps once every 6 months. This is also actually the ideal timeline to update your resume and LinkedIn profile

UNDERSTANDING PERSONALITIES

*T*rue story.

One of my best buddies from Engineering College, KK and I got placed in the same firm, one of the world's largest automobile makers in its Indian manufacturing operations. This having happened somewhere at the beginning of our last year in college, we had the whole year to conjure up images of how our workplace would be, what our roles would entail, and so on.

KK is the eternal extrovert to my incorrigible introvert. D-Day, the date of our joining came soon enough. Both of us boarded the Company bus from our respective pick- up points to travel the hour and fifteen minutes or so it took to reach the plant . Here is a first person, almost verbatim account of what transpired in KK's bus between him and the passenger next to him.

KK: So, I am KK, joining today

Neighbor (Half opening his eyes): Ok

KK: Which department do you work in ?

Neighbor: Production. The Vehicle Assembly Shop. I am an operator on the Assembly Line.

KK: Since how many years have you been here ?

Neighbor: (Still yawning) For the last 9 years.

KK: How does it feel to work for the World's Largest Automobile firm , renowned for its management philosophies, and outstanding quality of vehicles and blah blah blah blah ???

Neighbor: Boss, I have been on the Production line for the last 9 years, for 8 hours every day, doing more or less the same work. I have no feelings left.

While the above sentiment is true for many a worker, prodded by the monotony and impersonalization that the modern-day Production line inherently demands, the same lack of feelings is definitely not exhibited by anyone involved in either the admits or the offers process. Admissions and Talent hunting are extremely humanized activities and often involve inexact sciences, less than accurate data gathering and analysis, and hence haphazard decision-making processes.

What I strive to achieve through this chapter is to offer a glimpse of what's going on in the stakeholder's mind and consequent to this, what the candidate must and must not do to make her/his case more compelling.

The psyche of a recruiter
What the recruiter is typically going through

Consider the following things when thinking of your primary audience for your resume, the recruiter:

- She/he may not read your resume for more than a minute.
- She/he typically has an attention span of less than 15 seconds.
- She/ he might be new to the industry you are coming from or are applying to, so all the fancy jargon you have so proudly stamped on your resume might have zero chance of registering in the minds.
- Your resume might be the 100th that she/he is reading for the day, and every one of the preceding 99 might have elicited the same word cloud in her foggy brain. Worst case, your resume is picked up right after a heavy lunch!
- Topping up on the previous point, yours is the 100th resume for the same job posting.
- After all the 100 resumes or so have been perused, and your resume is among the 10 or so shortlisted, the recruiter might have to convince her/his boss as well as the hiring manager that these 10 resumes were indeed worthy of selection.
- Out of the 10, the boss/ hiring manager might pick up only half or less in order to schedule interviews, as everyone has limited time slots available. You need to ensure that you are additionally qualified for this shortlist among the shortlisted candidates.
- The recruiter might decide to use some form of automation through software, which sifts through the haystack of resumes and applications.

What the recruiter wants from you

- Content that is easy on the eye and can be quickly understood at first glance. Declutter your resume and keep cleaning to ensure that someone else who is reading
- Content available in a standard, prescribed format or one that is easy to understand. Also, having keywords which you indeed can claim to have an association with and are also mentioned in the job description
- It is great to have resumes which can be summarized and associated through a single phrase. For example:- Aniketh, the State 10th Boards topper, or Sharath, the mountaineer. Strive to have this one positive associated either through your academics, work experience, or extra-curriculars. In fact, I believe this is the only use of having any extra curricular activities mentioned in your resume.
- Only relevant things are on the resume. For example, your father's name or the declaration that everything you write on this resume is true to the best of your knowledge. The former is irrelevant in that, gone are the days in which you will get a job because of who your father is and the latter is redundant because, by sharing the resume, you implicitly make the declaration.

What the recruiter does not want from you

- Specifying further on relevance, the recruiter would not want to see non-relevant information. Some examples of non-relevance, according to me are
    - If you are an engineer applying for a finance role after an MBA which was preceded by 4 years of heavy engineering work,

much of the technical nuances of how you achieved those objectives in the engineering role would be non-relevant.
    o Events from way back in the past, like the fact that you participated in a swimming competition 15 years ago and managed a participation certificate.
- Lying on the resume. Background checks happen more often than you think they do
- Fancy, non-coherent jargon (also mentioned at the beginning of this section).
- Really long essays. Word count is not the metric, clarity of communication is.

The psyche of a hiring manager

What the Hiring Manager is typically going through

The hiring manager, unlike the recruiter, is not solely focused on the recruiting process. This is just one among many competing priorities for the manager.

- Unless and until a key role has witnessed attrition and needs to be urgently filled up, recruiting is an activity undertaken for future time periods. It can be taken for sure to not be a Must-complete task but a Good-to-complete one.
- The recruiting manager is universally the creator of the job requirement and hence the job description. Usually, he/she has perhaps between 50% to 80% of clarity in terms of what the job is, and what kind of profile is required to perform the job.
- Both the upside of a good hire and the downside of a bad hire are very difficult to evaluate and will take time in most cases. This means that it is very seldom that the hiring manager is held accountable for the quality of the hiring process.
- Time and inherent attention span are both scarce for the manager to be actively involved in the hiring process.

What the hiring manager wants from you

- The comments on clarity, jargon, and association still hold.
- Enough content in the resume and the application form for the manager to justify to both himself and his manager that the time spent on shortlisting your resume for further processes was worthwhile. The candidate does not even need to come across as spectacular, even safe ones pass through.

- A clear picture of what you achieved in your previous roles and how you achieved them.
- What the manager sees in the resume in written form should tally with what and how you speak during the interviewing process.

What the hiring manager does not want from you

- Everything in the section about what recruiters don't want
- Lying on the resume. Background checks happen more often than you think they do. Emphasized enough.
- Ambiguity about whether or not to proceed with a candidature.

The psyche of a professor reviewing admissions
What the Professor is typically going through

The popular image of many a professor/teacher who operates at the Post Graduate level is as a nerdy teacher, beloved to students and oblivious to the rest of the world as he/she is involved in teaching and research.

This is an outdated image. The modern-day College Professor in many ways has the autonomy of a CEO, the skills of a polymath, and the schedule of a Head of State. The different roles that he plays are as follows: teacher, researcher, publisher of research, consultant in his area of expertise, administrator of varying responsibilities, and additionally a key member of the household. Added to this are the stresses of getting tenure (if not already tenured), the cutthroat competition of the academic world, and the politics of the School.

To sum it all up, the professor is a very busy man. Admissions occupy perhaps 5% of his overall responsibility and up to 10% of the schedule in his calendar. There are stringent timelines to be adhered to and within this timeline, a fair admission process must be administered and seen to be administered. The professor is closeted with other committee members for many a day during the shortlisting and needs to travel frequently during the interview sessions. I am pretty sure that the rest of the above-mentioned responsibilities do not pause during the Interview season.

Additionally, please remember that the professor interacts with hundreds of students every year and his point of reference about any character or trait he wants to see in a prospective student has a very large sample size and hence his opinions are very grounded.

What the Professors want from you

Whether it be a written application or essay or face-to-face interviews and group discussions, the Professors want to see from their candidates the following

- Above average, or better intelligence. They know that not all students are gifted and many can cut their grades and make up for lesser intelligence through sheer hard work and diligence.
- Clarity in both written submissions and during verbal interactions. Always operate under the worst-case assumption that the Professor sees your entire application package for maybe 5 minutes before you enter the interview room. Can your presentation give a crisp, consistent, and coherent picture in those 5 minutes? That is the litmus test for the quality of your preparation.
- Learnability- Any evidence that you are an active and continuous learner of varying topics within or beyond academics is seen as very positive in your candidature.
- Coachability- After all, if the candidate is not coachable, what is the point of spending all the time in the course trying to learn new things? This trait is particularly tested during the interviews as professors often interject with advice and see how such advice is received and processed by candidates.
- Composure- The candidate should not get rattled when stress tested. Can the candidate further withstand cold calling in the classroom?
- Additionally, is the candidate interesting? Some of the unique candidates I have come across or heard about in my Business School are a Police Officer (my classmate) and a Miss India winner (a junior in the 2-year program). These

kinds of candidates bring very interesting, unique, and maybe entertaining insights to the classroom and the learning.

What the Professors do not want from you

- A know-it-all. If you show such behavio r, what are the chances that you are going to attempt to learn anything in the classroom?
- Being too timid or shy- At the postgraduate level, students are expected to be very articulate in the classroom and participate actively. Shyness is a huge barrier.
- The opposite of the above; someone who indulges in what we used to call in IIM Ahmedabad as DCP (Desperate Class participation).

The psyche of an Admissions officer
What the Admissions Office/Officer is typically going through

The Admissions officer, in a typical admissions process has two things and only two things to do. Select and eliminate. Understanding the key differences between the two requirements is one of the most critical aspects of your admission journey.

Selection is about creating a broad profile of a desirable candidate or an entire cohort of candidates, depending on the kind of program. There are some programs like MBAs where the biggest learning often derives from the diversity of the candidates and the peer learning this drives. In other programs like a PhD in Computer Engineering, the requirement is for a candidate to have a Bachelor's Degree and preferably a Master's Degree in the same subject and some relevant work experience.

The Admissions Committee first creates this profile and defines its contour through different parameters like educational qualification, standardiz ed test scores, work experience, and other factors like diversity and extracurriculars. They then communicate the profile through road shows and online media like webinars and the School's website to ensure that they reach the widest possible net of candidates.

The actual admissions process for them is then a mixture of further selection and elimination, primarily depending on the number of rounds that they can plan and execute and the size of the funnel passing through each of these rounds.

Consider this. A fairly long application form for admission and a not inexpensive application fee is by itself a process of elimination as only the really genuine candidates will then take an interest and apply/pay. Further, admission cut-offs on different parameters also tend to eliminate a bulk of the candidates.

During all of this, certain requirements are expected of the Admissions team and its officers.

First of all, they are expected to fully fill up the seats! This does not seem like a point of conversation for reputed programs in a country like India, but it is good to keep this point at the back of your mind for a very good reason. Remember that every seat unfilled is an opportunity to earn revenue for the school that has been missed. Hence, it naturally assumes that, as much as the candidate covets the admission, the admissions office desires to fill its seats with candidates who can complete the program and also increase the brand of the School as alumni.

The Admissions office needs to be fair as well as perceived to be fair. In this context, it is in the rarest of the rare cases that any candidate would have a marginal benefit over others in the form of clandestine support of the Admissions office.

Because the Admissions office is selecting against a profile, the single biggest benefit of this is the access to information that is implicitly available to the smart and diligent candidate who takes the effort to look through data on admission demographics from previous batches. Admissions is one of the few areas where history can be used for a reliable forecast, not at an individual level but at the level of the entire class.

Because of the sheer volume of applications that the Admissions Office has perused every year, they know that it pays to have a holistic look at the candidate, who might have low academic scores previously but might show traits of tenacity and discipline elsewhere which might bode well for performance in this score. Thank God AI is not involved, or is Chat GPT already being trained to look for the intangible but interesting snippet of information?

What the Admissions Office wants from you

Think of the Admissions Office as both a key decision-maker and a decision enabler. In this context, the following are supercritical:

- Clarity and comprehensiveness in submissions. Do not make the Admissions Committee reach out to you repeatedly. In the flow of huge quantities of applications, they might forget to reach out to you for clarifications or incorporate the clarifications you have already provided.
- Single phrase associations, which have already been outlined above are useful though to a lesser extent.
- Data that is truthful and can be verified easily through background checks.

What the Admissions Office does not want from you

- Unwanted information. This is of zero use.
- Frequent follow-ups to check on the status. If there is something worth notifying, the Admissions Committee will indeed take the trouble and reach out to you !

- Single phrase associations, which have already been outlined above are useful though to a lesser extent.
- Data that is truthful and can be verified easily through background checks.

SELLING YOURSELF

The Art and Science of Selling Yourself

No matter what you do in life, one skill is essential to succeed in the workplace. Selling yourself. Selling to your parents, a partner, your teachers, colleagues, children, clients, and so on. The paradox is that not even the best business schools teach you how to sell. Then, there is that big debate, universal across many others of whether you are born a salesman or get trained to be one. I believe that the answer lies on both sides.

My one- liner on this topic:- Sell yourself in every conversation by providing a crisp, clear, and coherent communication which is positive in nature to the relevant audience.

The long form of this, for the limited scope of selling oneself in the context of admits and offers will take several pages to elaborate. The below framework would suit us here. I assure you that answering the below questions by yourself , preferably by writing them down will help you way further than any amount of preparation on the topic.

1. Who is the audience ?
2. What are you trying to convey to them and what do you intend to get from this conversation?
3. What are the aspects of this conversation that are in your control and hence the areas you should focus on ?
4. As an antithesis to the above, what are the aspects that are not in your control and hence you should not focus on ?

Who is the audience ?

Make a list of the people who are part of your intended communication; whether written or through face-to-face meetings physically or virtually. If you do not know, make an educated guess about the personality trait of the person you are communicating with .

You should be actively using LinkedI n at a minimum and maybe other social media like Facebook, Instagram, Youtube, and X to find out if this person has written stuff or posted content that provides a glimpse into the mindset. This will also make you more comfortable with their voice, their body language, and any jargon/ phrases that might be typical of them.

The previous chapter on *Understanding Personalities* was a template to impress upon you that there is a great deal of insight to be gained if we spend some time on this exercise.

Some key questions to keep in mind are

(Straight from the previous chapter)

1. What is the person going through ?
2. What does that person want from you ?
3. What does that person not want from you ?

Additionally,

4. How familiar is that person with you and vice versa ?
5. How familiar is the person with the topic of conversation ?
6. Do they have agendas beyond the scope of your engagement that you should be aware of ?
7. Does the person have a superior bargaining position over you ?

What are you trying to convey to them and what do you intend to get out of this conversation ?

There is a popular belief that any communication is meant to achieve at least one or more of the following: Impress, Motivate, Entertain, Teach, or Change.

In the context of our discussion on admits and offers, I believe that the critical areas of focus are

a. **Teach** the audience about you as a person, with all your unique skills and accomplishments. However, brevity is important here and they do need to know the minutest of details about you from some 15 years ago.
b. **Impress** the audience about your relevance and suitability for an academic program or a job role
c. Perhaps, **Entertain** by writing with flair and well-deliberated wit.

Also, do not attempt the following

a. Beg, plead, or pray about anything. No matter how you feel, you are not in an inferior bargaining position in any of these transactions.
b. Comments about the admission or interview process in a cycle where the candidate is applying have zero chance of being acknowledged or accepted. Once, a candidate for a B-School with a background in the Education Sector and otherwise stellar credentials told me that he had spent half a page on his essay topic of "*How you are going to uniquely contribute to the classroom*" by writing about how he will change the teaching methodology. Needless to say, he did not even receive an interview call !
c. Do not spend time praising the audience (like Professors, for example). More often than not, this is easily discernible, appears shallow, and has a high likelihood of not being well received.

What are the aspects of this engagement that are in your control and hence your focus areas ?

The basic premise of this section and the next is the belief that time and energy are limited resources and should be spent only on areas where we hold sway.

We start with self- identity. The way we think and the stories we tell inwardly about ourselves are thence manifested to the outer world in part or in full. Hence, it is absolutely critical that we hold ourselves in esteem, and work with the belief that the world will become a better place for us provided we use a combination of talent, hard work, and luck.

Things to be wary of are The Dunning-Kruger Effect and its partial antithesis (at least for the initial portion of the Dunning-Kruger Curve), the Imposter Syndrome. Both are detrimental in very different ways. Whereas the former provides a false sense of confidence, the latter deters even good candidates from even trying out for a job or an admit.

Our understanding of the course outline or the job description is in enough depth to roughly determine whether we are suitable as well as interested in the course or the job.

The way we visualize and represent our previous academics and work experience. This can be presented as blandly as a seemingly unending chronology of events as recorded in an accounting ledger or can be picturized as an exciting journey of learning, discovery, achievements, and service to various causes.

The formal submissions we make. Are they done in a clean, timely, and legible manner, bereft of mistakes, grammatical or otherwise ? Are they comprehensive in nature ? Do these submissions show the true professional that we are ?

Do we have a coherent, if not complete picture of what the future looks like for us ? Do we have a hypothesis of what it takes to get there ?

What are the aspects of this conversation that are not in your control and hence the areas you should ignore ?

The quantity and caliber of the competition. In countries like India and China, where inevitably many candidates of equal stature compete for few seats or jobs, it is detrimental to even think about the candidate pool. In this aspect, it is highly recommended to remain completely oblivious to the size of the pool and only focus on the admit or the offer.

How any one or more candidates are stacked up against you and are faring in the process? Again, this line of thought has zero utility in my opinion, and only serves to increase your anxiety and feeling of helpfulness. Also, it is unfair to the other candidate(s) as well as you never know the entire gamut of their own journey.

Thoughts about whether the process is fair or not and whether you will be one of its victims. Unless gross injustice is being openly carried out, it is always better to assume that the selection and elimination processes for admits or offers are fair to all and nobody's looking to actively target you. Everyone might have biases but let us assume that the biases will not unjustly deny you of what is rightfully yours.

What is the definition of success ?

The outcome of most college and job selection processes is tangible and has intermediate stages. This can be intuitive for most but it is still valuable to carry out this exercise of spelling out how success is defined.

As an illustrative example, consider the IIMA PGPX admission process. Essays are sought from students shortlisted for the Personal interview by a faculty member. A narrow definition of success in this round might be something like submitting the essays within a specified timeline. However, stretch a little further and you can easily visualize that the essay is one important frame of reference for the faculty about you as a candidate before they call you in for the interview. Hence, it is imperative that there is a syncing of the essay with your resume and what you are preparing for the interview.

Additionally, is the essay also a feeder to the decision- making process on scholarships ? If so, have you made enough references to points which are helpful to evaluate your suitability based on merit and/or financial need ? Before starting on any aspect of an application, please note down what you think might be both the stated and unstated goals of that aspect or submission.

Based on your thorough evaluation of the replies to the above 4 questions on selling yourself, you are now ready for the tactical work ahead. The actual submissions themselves vary but can be broadly listed, summarized, and studied in depth.

The next sections of this chapter focus on the nuts and bolts of the different aspects of the admit and offer process. I have pasted for reference inside the relevant portions of the section my own documents like resumes and cover letters, which are the actual ones I've used in different situations. I hope they sufficiently illustrate the specific points I intend to convey.

Resume

The Golden Rule is a tenet found across religious and socially significant books in Ancient India, Greece, and Egypt. Simply put, it says to treat others the way you want them to treat you. In its negative or prohibitive form, it says to not treat others the way you do not want them to treat you. This, to me, is a great way to think about resumes. Do not write a resume that you would not want to read.

An effective way to do this is to consider your resume as a very expensive piece of real estate, not to be wasted at the very least. A majority of the resumes I come across seem to have a diametrically opposite point of view, more akin to the kind of tactics that we were used to in engineering colleges; the more we write, the more marks we get.

Maybe it has got to do with this digital medium where it costs no one to write an extra page of resume on a word processor like MS Word. However, this is totally wrong in my opinion as we are looking at storage space as the resource in question. It is, in fact, the attention of the reader.

In order to consider this, it is useful to know how the human mind perceives data and visualization. Here are some perceptions, according to me.

- Most of us who use English as the primary medium of business communication are inherently accustomed to writing from left to right and from top to bottom. Hence, it naturally follows that the most important things that we write should be at the top and to the left of our resume.

- Paragraphs are harder to read and it is always better to use bulleted lists.
- On any topic, if you want to elaborate on the bullet points, try to contain the bullets between a minimum of three and to maximum of five. Any more than this and the probability that you've lost the reader's attention skyrockets.
- Maintain either the Active Voice or the Passive voice throughout the resume. Active voice is preferred.
- What is highlighted using Bold, Italic, and underlined gets immediate attention. Make full use of this to get the readers to focus their attention where you think is necessary.
- The human mind, when presented with non-standard data, gets confused very quickly. The best way to mitigate this is to have a standardized template where there is a place for everything and everything is in its place.

I have found that it is most convenient to have one long master resume-two or three pages, and to distill and condense it further into a 1- page resume as is required for a particular job description. Also, please keep in mind that you should know the implications of every single word on your resume and take responsibility for everything written here.

Below are considerations for different segments of a resume. Each of these is appended with a segment of the most recent resume that I have used to successfully get a job offer. Not all of what I have recommended is necessarily available in my resume, that does not dilute the recommendation though.

Summary

- At the very top, make sure to have your primary contact details listed. An email ID, a phone number, and a link to your profile on LinkedI n or a personal web page that details key projects should suffice.
- Basic details like the number of years of experience, industries, and companies along with your highest qualification should be listed. If you feel that the firms you have been associated with or the schools you went to are prominent in the minds of the reader, please do mention their names and highlight them.
- Devote one line to top roles and if required, the major achievements in these roles.
- Skills can either be mentioned in a single line or in a separate table.
- Write about your ambitions in at least the short to mid-term time frame.
- In essence, the summary indicates clearly to the reader whether your resume is relevant enough to continue reading for their consideration.

ANIRUDDHA MYSORE SRINATH

x16aniruddha@iima.ac.in +91 9535022111 Linkedin #12, SBI Prime Residency, Kodichikkanahalli, Bengaluru 560076

PROFILE

Management Professional with **12 years** of experience and a focus on **planning and execution of new initiatives**, primarily in the **Manufacturing** Space.

Have worked in the **Automotive (EV & IC Engines)** and Aerospace Industries with firms **like Ola Electric, Ather Energy, Cyient Limited** and Toyota Motor Corporation.

Possess two full time Master's Degrees, an **MBA from the Indian Institute of Management, Ahmedabad** and a **Master's Degree in Manufacturing** from the University of Michigan, Ann Arbor.

Keen on pursuing roles in Manufacturing Strategy and Operations

SKILLS

• Electric Vehicles/ Battery/ Cell Technology	• Manufacturing Execution Systems and Industry 4.0
• Greenfield Plant Setup and Start of Operations	• Business Model Canvas
• Manufacturing Systems- Process Design	• Technology Road mapping

Work Profile

(Lengthy list alert !)

- The sequencing of the Work Profile and the Education section should be considered based on which is the current or the immediate past activity you have pursued between the two. Or, if one is so overwhelmingly impressive that it has to be put up first.
- List your work stints in reverse chronological order, earliest first.
- Please write the full name of the firm along with the year and month of start and end of tenure.
- In case the company is relatively unknown, write a short description of the Company's products and services, the regions that they operate in, and their size in terms of market capitalization or revenue and employee size.
- You should further classify the work into whatever logical sections you feel are right, based on usually geographical division, role division, or designation division. Anything is fine, but classifying is indeed important.
- At the start of each of these sections, write about your key responsibility.
- Mention what your achievement was and how you achieved it.
- List your roles and achievements in order of priority. A minimum of 3 up to a maximum of 5.
- Have numbers that make sense. Play between using absolute numbers and percentages, whichever is more impressive in your opinion.

- Use the metrics which are universal in your industry. For example, the manufacturing sector uses quality, cost, delivery, and safety.
- Please use the currency that is either used in the region where you worked or in the region where you are applying.
- Do not use any short form at all. Instead, use the full form. If you know that the person you are sending your resume to has little experience in the same sector, also add in parentheses what is the significance of that jargon.
- Motherhood opinions like working with Cross-Functional teams are of no use. Most business problems need to be solved with a cross-functional team and it's a waste of everybody's time to have something like this in your resume.
- As much as possible, try and have only one sentence per bullet point.

EXPERIENCE

Ola Electric Technologies, Bengaluru — May 2020- Present

- **Associate Director, Manufacturing**
    1. Lead for **Manufacturing Execution Systems (MES)** and **Industry 4.0**
        a) Leading design and Industrialization of industry 4.0/smart factory technologies for manufacturing lines of welding, assembly, material movement, battery and motor and building digitally integrated shop floor.
        b) Drive and establish complete integration between different manufacturing shops, Enterprise level systems, and implement Manufacturing Execution system (MES) across the shop floor.
    2. Lead for **Feasibility studies** on **manufacturing plans beyond the 2-Wheeler Factory**.
    3. Led **Initial Plant Masterplan Development** for Ola's Future Factory which will eventually have a capacity of **10 million**. In a highly **accelerated time frame of around 3 months**, helped develop the processes required to understand investments, manpower requirement, Major Shops and Block Layouts for initial capacity of 0.5 million
    4. **Finalized Vendors for 4 different Shops: - Weld, Paint, Assembly and Battery as well as for robots and AMRS**. The Vendor identification, qualification and award was completed in a highly compressed time frame of 4 months and with significant overlap with the master planning phase.
    5. Worked on **advanced scenarios and plans to ensure optimization of above plan for capacity and flexibility**.
    6. **Created the Manufacturing Organization.** Wrote all the Job Descriptions and conducted more than 200 interviews to **form the initial core team of around 25 Manufacturing professionals**.
    7. Led the Plan for **Hiring and Training of more than 1000 blue Collared Workers**.
    8. Initially, led all initiatives on **Manufacturing Strategy** and Footprint including Cost, Location Identification, Smart Manufacturing and Outsourcing decisions

Ather Energy Private Limited, Bengaluru — November 2017- May 2020

- **Deputy General Manager, Operations Strategy** — September 2018- May 2020
    1. Responsible for **Capacity and Capability Acquisition** through both **organic and inorganic** mechanisms and for Capacity Planning for Volume Ramping and New Model Introduction.
        a) Strategy Lead for Frameworks of decision making on **In-house Vs. Contract Manufacturing.**
            i. Lead for **new Facility in Hosur, Tamil Nadu** to cater to Manufacturing of Batteries and Vehicles. **Liaised with land developers and State Governments in South India** to negotiate the best terms, prices and subsidies.
    2. Established the **Ather Manufacturing Model** for Medium to Term Long Decisions on Operations Strategy.
    3. Managed the **EHS and Logistics** Functions
    4. Set up more than **50 business processes** required for Operations using tools like **SAP and JIRA**.
    5. Set up Operation Finance Frameworks and Control mechanisms including **financial MIS and budget tracking**.

- **Deputy General Manager, Manufacturing** — November 2017- August 2018
    1. **Designated Factory Manager** for Ather Energy's First Manufacturing Facility with a 70-member team
    2. Started and led the **Production, Production Engineering, Stores and Planning, Maintenance and EHS**
        a) **Commissioned the Factory in a Period of 8 months** and Ran Builds for Product and Process Validation and Pilot Production. Increased the **Factory Capacity by 10 times.**

Education

- The sequencing of education and work experience should be carefully considered.
- Usually a Bachelor's degree and later is good enough to list down. What you did or how much you scored in your Class 10 is of not much use after your graduation, unless you were Ranked #1 or 2 in your state.

- It is not necessary to write about your marks or grades at school. A good thumb rule would be to stop using grades beyond a year after you graduate from that course.
- Write about key projects that you pursued, what you learned , and where you did your project from. This is especially important for people with close to zero full- time work experience. For those with many years of experience, it is not even required to list these projects in my opinion as they would be completely shadowed by all the real- world stuff done.

EDUCATION

- PGPX- One Year Full Time MBA - Indian Institute of Management, Ahmedabad (Top Quartile) — 2016 - 2017
- Master in Engineering, Manufacturing- University of Michigan, Ann Arbor (USA) — 2012 - 2012
- Bachelor in Engineering, Mechanical- Bangalore Institute of Technology — 2003 - 2007

Extracurricular

- If you are a National Level athlete or have already acted in a Telegu movie that was a Rs. 100 crore blockbuster, your resume should have the extra curricular at the top of your summary.
- If it is anything less than this, please restrain yourself from writing too elaborate on this topic.
- As a rule, do not write about having participation certificates for different activities.
- What hobby you pursued might not have continued until and beyond the time you started working. Your more recent hobby might be binging on Netflix and stalking people on Instagram and Facebook. Be selective in what you write here, you might often end up getting grilled more on this section than on the one about work experience !

MISCELLANEOUS

1. Have won the top Performer awards at Ola Electric (Most Valued Performer, FY-2021), Ather (First Among Equals- FY 2018) in 2018 and Cyient (Mark of Excellence- FY 2014)
2. **Coordinator** for the **Speaker Series Committee** at IIM Ahmedabad for the PGPX 2016-17 Batch
3. **Mentor** for **Prospective and Current MBA** students at GoCrackit. Help and advice students over the full life-cycle of MBA course like **mock interviews, resume and application review and career advice.**
4. Regular Blogger published at https://aniruddhams.com/. I usually blog on technology policy and careers

LinkedIn Profile

If the resume is a short story, the LinkedIn profile is an epic novel.

Offering a large canvas in which to discover, showcase, collaborate, and create on a variety of career- related topics, LinkedI n can be the most powerful medium and/or tool in your arsenal. I have used it to connect with friends, both old and new, find jobs, read content, and journal my professional and academic journey.

As with any modern social medium, this one too has its attractions and distractions. On the latter, think trolls, mindless debates, jingoism, fake influencers, and fake identities. Brushing aside all of these, the attractions are innumerable. Let me list down a few,

- The connections. The known, the unknown, and the aspirational. From your colleges and firms that you have gone to and want to go to. Much of the jobs that I have been offered over the last 10 years have been through connections that I have maintained through LinkedI n. And much of the content I have poured into this book has been through the conversations with people, most of whom have connected with me on this medium.
- The jobs themselves. With detailed job descriptions, an insight into how many people have applied and their demographics. And with recommendations based on profile and interest.

- The content posted by others is marginally useful, in my opinion. The written word, surveys, videos, and infographics. This is where all the distractions occur. However, I believe that the noise levels are way lower than in other media.
- The content that you post is bound to be more useful as it provides you with the confidence to create and publish, obtain quick validation as well achieve fame within the confines of this population.
- Creating and maintaining your professional & academic profile is also useful as LinkedI n is user- friendly from an editing perspective as well as offers the ability to save your profile as a pdf, hence making for an excellent supplement for a longish resume, in case such a thing is required.

In my segment- wise analysis of a LinkedI n Profile, I will attempt to skip the points I have already mentioned about resumes so that the advice is not made redundant.

Profile Snapshot

- First and foremost, choose a profile picture which bears a close resemblance to how you currently look ! It has to be non casual, if not formal, and candid pictures are definitely not appealing though they might be entertaining. Background photos are also encouraged but not mandatory, make them relevant to your personality.
- Choose a summary that you would want people to remember you by. Consider it your personalized elevator pitch. It is usually a good practice to include the most prominent element of your profile here. Like that Fortune 100 company you work(ed) for,

the elite school that you went to, or a skill where you have a Shaolin master level of expertise.
- The callouts on your workplace and the last school that you went to appear automatically from these relevant sections.
- Do add your contact information. Usually, an email ID being actively used is sufficient. Consider that your contact details might be seen by many, many people, and hence providing a mobile number might solicit a ton of unwanted spam messages and calls, which are easier to ignore if via mail.
- If you are actively open to work, LinkedI n enables you to prominently display this and other statuses.

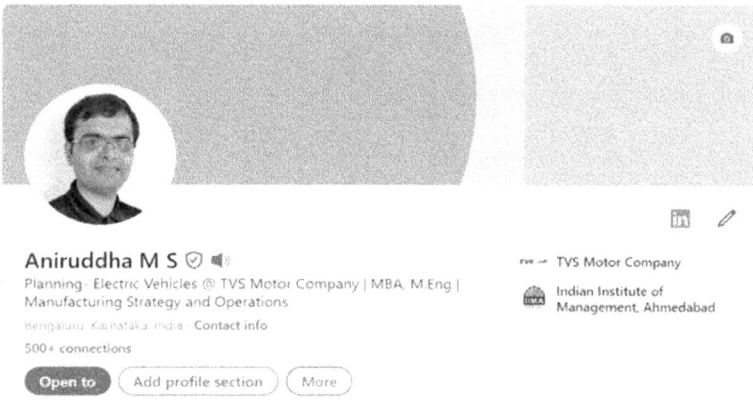

About

- This section is a 2- minute read into your profile, where the reader gets to understand a little bit more about the professional and the person that you are.
- Use either short paragraphs or bulleted points not exceeding a single line.

- Again, highlight the most important elements of your profile succinctly.
- Provide a link to other places where your work might be portrayed. Medium, Gitbhub, etc
- Highlight the top skills that you possess.
- Use LinkedI n- powered AI generation solutions to further condense and refine this section. I have recently started using this solution and can vouch for the results.

About

I am a Lead Planner for Electric Vehicles at TVS Motor, with 14 years of experience in the planning and execution of new initiatives in advanced manufacturing. I have an MBA from IIM Ahmedabad, a Master in Engineering from University of Michigan, and a Graduate Certificate in Technology Policy from Takshashila Institution.

My core competencies include operations, strategy, government engagement, business development, and project management. I have worked with leading organizations in the automotive and aerospace industries, such as Ola Electric, Ather Energy, IBM, Cyient, and Toyota. I have also received top performance awards in the first year of my stint for three of the firms I have worked with. I am passionate about technology, blogging, and yoga.

I write on the Medium Platform : https://medium.com/@x16aniruddha

Top skills
Operations Management • Electric Vehicles • Manufacturing Strategy • Manufacturing Start-Up

Work Experience

- The chronology is straightforward and as it should be; your most recent experience is of most relevance to everybody and it appears first.
- Based on whether you are aiming for expertise or climbing the ladder, choose your job titles respectively. In my case, I am at a point right now where I am keen to pursue a couple of experiences I have never had in my career so my resume does not show the progressive levels of seniority I have achieved but instead shows the different roles I have performed.

- There is an excellent opportunity in this section to add relevant visual media that showcase your work. For example, I was part of a team that built a new plant for one of the earlier firms I had worked in. I used the video clip of a news report that showed the inauguration of the new plant and highlighted the equipment I had worked on. People who have digital portfolios can really exploit this feature.
- Also, the skills tagged by you in a later section come with an accompanying question of when you learned or exhibited them, and this gets captured in this section.

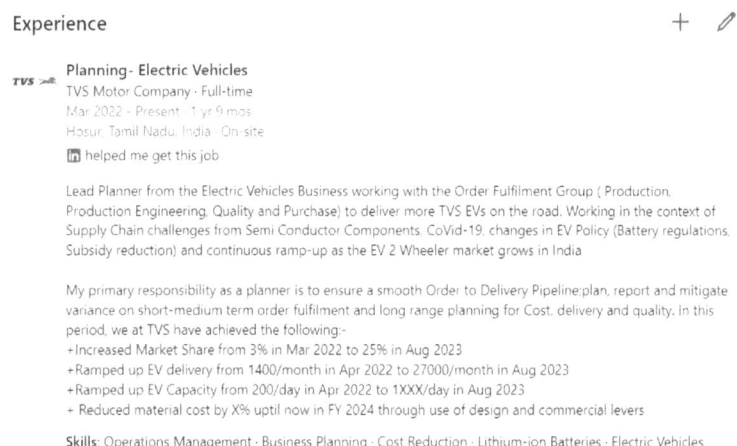

Education

- Though I state in the resume portion that it is enough to show education from high school onwards, I would make it a point to have education experiences shown on LinkedIn to stretch till the beginning of school. For the simple reason that friends from even primary school would form a great network and you should give these friends a chance to search for you.

- The opinions on using visual media and skills remain the same from the previous portion on work experience.
- I have recently started seeing profiles where people do not mention their timeline of attending different schools. Trying to hide your age ? I don't know what benefit this is going to have as people can deduce anyway, at least the year in which you finished your undergraduate degree.
- Even though it is good to always write education in chronological order, I also believe in the merit of highlighting the schools in your list which have the best pedigree and also the ones which you attended full- time. This can be done by dragging these to the very top.

Education   + ✎

Indian Institute of Management Ahmedabad
PGPX, MBA
2016 - 2017
Activities and societies: Co-ordinator, Speaker Series Committee
Reviewer, Gandhian Young Technology Innovation Award: 2017
Member, Manufacturing Club

The PGPX Program is IIMA's one year full time MBA. It is ranked among the top 30 MBA programs in the World by Financial Times in its 2017 rankings.
https://www.iima.ac.in/web/pgpx

Extracurriculars: Projects, Publications, licenses and certifications, Honors and awards

- Use these sections to also tag the people or the institutes that you have collaborated with.
- If required, add relevant links to other websites where your certificates and licenses are available.

Admits and Offers

← **Projects** +

Analyzing a Clean tech start-up for position for value capture and investability
Dec 2012 - Present

Ⓜ Associated with University of Michigan

(Show project ↗)

Worked on repositioning of an Australian Company, which was a spin-off from University Research and working on materials for silicon wafers

Other contributors

← **Publications** + ✎

Why the time is now for 3D printing in the medical world- part 1
http://healthcareinnovationmonitor.com/ · Apr 21, 2016

(Show publication ↗)

Written when I was still in Cyient :)

Other authors

← **Licenses & certifications** +

edX Professional Certificate in Electric Cars offered by Delft University
edX
Issued Nov 2019
Credential ID 1e5d3530d5784fd98131a70b181b16f1

(Show credential ↗)

coursera Digital Manufacturing & Design Technology Specialization offered by State University of New York, Buffalo
Coursera
Issued Jan 2019
Credential ID 2UNQXEK2ELBF

(Show credential ↗)

80

Recommendations

- Recommendations are a great public endorsement, with context and details of your work from the people whom you've worked with. Make sure to have at least one recommendation from every job stint you have or every course you have undertaken.
- At work, it would be great to get Linkedin recommendations from your direct supervisors. Of course it goes without saying that you have to put in the work and maintain the relationship with your supervisor that is required to get the recommendation.
- Ensure that your recommenders provide specific context and situations of where they have worked with you and thence their opinion of you.

Standardized Tests

You cannot create experience. You have to undergo it.

Albert Camus

As per my rough estimates, standardized tests occupy between 40% and 60% weightage in any application process. However, I feel that most applicants give them between 80% and 100% of their time and attention, often neglecting other important facets like the resume, essays, and interviews. Nevertheless, even 40% is significant so let us spend some time discussing tests.

There are many tutors who work extensively with standardized test seekers. Almost all of those who I know make it an annual ritual to write the standardized test that they tutor for, themselves. Though I do not write as frequently, the number of standardized tests I have taken for post graduate level seems ridiculous to many, many people who know me. Below is my personal disclosure of test scores. I think they are in the range of average to above average. They were enough to get me an admit and that's all that matters.

GRE		GMAT		
March 2006	December 2009	Oct 2010	June 2011	August 2015
1270/1600	1430/1600	710/800	680/800	710/800

The reasons that I have written the GRE and GMAT so many times ? The usual suspects. Wanting to improve my scores. Not sure what course to apply to so let's keep all avenues open. Scores have expired so I need to rewrite.

My one line of wisdom, quite ubiquitous, is the following. A standardized test is a measure of how well you take that standardized test; nothing more and nothing else. Indian tests, global tests; all the same. However, the key difference in my opinion and the one which candidates should pay the most attention to is the scoring algorithm.

A test like the CAT, GATE, or XAT might have a linear scoring model. For example; 1 mark for a right answer, -0.25 marks for a wrong answer. Hence, the total score is (1 x number of right answers) + (-0.25 x number of wrong answers). Maybe there is a small penalty for unanswered questions, maybe not. The Math and verbal sections might have further sub-sections and you may need to score a minimum in each subsection.

Both the GRE and the GMAT work on an adaptive scoring algorithm. The explanation goes like this. The test starts with the assumption that you are an average candidate. For an illustrative (but not necessarily factually accurate) example, the GMAT starts with your score of 400. If you answer the first question right, it will add 100 points. The second answer, which is a bit more difficult question, will bump your score by 70 points to 570 if answered right.

Successive right answers will give diminishing deltas and the algorithm will come to an opinion about your scoring level. After a while, the questions also seem to get easier. The opposite is also true; a bad start with a couple of successive wrong answers will make your score plummet and stay there, no matter how many questions you will successively get right later on.

This has a lot of implications for the way you would approach a GMAT vs a linear test, say a CAT. In the CAT, you would pick up the questions you are most confident about in each section or subsection and race against time to compete. In the GMAT, you would be careful about how you pursue the first 5 to 10 questions as they are the most critical.

Many GMAT test takers also get disheartened when they see tough questions but do not realize that the reason for the question being tougher would be that the previous question was answered correctly. However, you would not be able to spend unreasonable amounts of time on the first few questions as there is also a penalty for not completing the test.

Which test to write ? Most schools help you take this thinking off your plate by specifying what scores they accept. In case you have a choice between two tests, always take the test which you think you have a better chance of performing on. I am a hundred percent convinced that no admissions office, having already provided options, will be biased for or against a choice.

How many times to write in the same admissions cycle ? I would recommend to plan for no more than one retakes if you are not happy and have a valid reason for not having a good score the first time and feel that things will be different the next time. Any attempt beyond the second is not bound to give you a major improvement in your score. Also, if you are apprehensive about how the college will judge you about having to retry, all colleges only consider your best score and there are no penalties in the final tally based on your number of attempts.

I recollect that my only serious preparation for these above tests was in the second GRE attempt for which I dedicated almost 2 hours every day for around 4 months. Everything else was at best a part- time, one- month effort. A rough estimate for preparation for someone who is writing a standardized test for the first time is around 10-12 hours a week for around 12 weeks.

How should you spend these 12 weeks ? Here is a rough idea.

Week 1	Week 2	Week 3	Week 4	Week 5	Week 6	Week 7	Week 8	Week 9	Week 10	Week 11	Week 12
Understanding the Pattern of the test											
		Understanding the topics of the test- Solving Easy Problem									
					Understanding the topics of the test- Solving difficult Problems						
Practice Test-1 Easy Level		Practice Test-2 Easy Level		Practice Test-3 Medium Level		Practice Test-4 Medium Level			Practice Test-5 Hard Level	Practice Test-6 Easy Level	Practice Test-7 Easy Level

As I have highlighted above, it is critical to understand the pattern of the test and the first couple of weeks should be spent towards that effort. Every test will primarily have these broad sections; mental aptitude, verbal comprehension, critical reasoning, and writing skills. The next 4 to 5 weeks should be spent in understanding these and solving easy topics. The subsequent month can be spent solving more difficult problems.

The last 2-3 weeks should not, at all, be spent in understanding topics in my opinion. This is a sure- shot way of inducing fatigue on oneself. Increase the level of testing every 2 weeks until the last few tests are really hard, at least 40-50% harder than the actual test itself. Every test should be followed by a thorough analysis of the sections where performance is not up to the mark and if at all any preparation is done, it needs to be done towards this.

For basic preparation, go for the books published by the test takers. They are for sure going to give you the most relevant information on the test itself apart from providing at least a couple of tests. You should ideally be picking up one more publisher for more problems to solve and something which offers between 4 to 6 free practice tests, ideally between medium to hard difficulty levels. I don't have recommendations for any particular test preparation brand.

Avoid the temptation of spending too much time preparing on any one section of the test to the peril of the balance of overall test preparation. Whether any section is a strength or weakness, make sure that a roughly equal amount of time is spent. This helps you avoid wasting time.

Statement of Purpose/ Cover Letter

What a Statement of Purpose (SOP) is to an Academic application, the Cover letter is to a job application. These documents are helpful to you in the following ways:

- Especially when it is not asked for, preparing and sending an SOP/ cover letter signals to the reader that you are willing to go beyond the application form to secure the job. This shows the right kind of initiative.
- It gives you the opportunity to be more creative than you can be with a regular application form or a resume, where you have to adhere to tightly laid standards and cannot weave stories.
- For people who are applying with a background different from the job description or the course, it provides an opportunity to elaborate on why you are keen on the job/ course and how you have skills that can be extended or transferable.
- It also provides the reader with the means to understand how well you understand the job description or the course.

At the end of this section, I will affix one SOP and one cover letter which were submitted by me, both of which have resulted in me getting an admit and an offer respectively. I have mostly used 2~3 page documents, I think anywhere between 1 and 3 pages is optimal. Please note that like in other documents of mine which I have affixed, all of what I have advocated below would not necessarily be available. This is because these documents are much more dated in terms of when they were actually used. They were the output of my collective wisdom at that time.

Introduction

- The introduction should be between 1 to 2 paragraphs, occupying no more than half a page.
- Many people, including me have used famous quotes to start with the introduction. This is fine, only make sure that the quote is neither cliched nor corny when read by someone else !
- The SOP/ cover letter should mention the role or the course for which you are applying, as the evaluator might be evaluating multiple applications at the same time.
- Very succinctly mention how your education till now, your current experience, or something in the immediate past overlaps with the job description or the course to which you are applying.
- Also state why you are keen on this course/role. It could be the problems to be solved, the skills to be acquired, the people you want to be associated with, or the location.

Body

- The body should contain 4 to 6 paragraphs, occupying between one and two pages.
- Use a combination of paragraphs and bullet points.
- Two distinct story lines need to be represented in this portion, one following the other.
  - The first storyline is a chronology of your academic career and your job stints, in the same order that they occurred, along with the major responsibilities that you have taken up in the job stints.
  - The second is a storyline of the top 2 to 3 skills that you believe distinguish you from other applicants. Depending

on what is the actual case, you may either show breadth of experience and education, thus indicating an inclination towards generalization, or depth, indicating specialization. Major projects that you have undertaken can also be mentioned and the STAR approach used to elaborate.
- As mentioned elsewhere, use between 3 to 5 bullet points in any paragraph to provide an illustration in any one of the two story lines.
- As in resumes, use all the 3 major highlights- **Bold**, *Italic,* and underline to good effect to call out the attention of the readers.
- A common mistake that people make, as in a resume, is to not distinguish between their team and themselves in terms of responsibilities and achievements. Separately call out both wherever responsibilities and achievements are being written about.

Conclusion

- The Conclusion should ideally be not more than a paragraph.
- It should highlight again the key reason that you are excited about the role/ course.
- In a line or two, quoting from highlights of the Body, it should illustrate why you believe that you are the perfect applicant.
- Thank the institution/ organization for the opportunity to apply and mention that you are looking forward to getting a positive outcome.

Statement of Purpose
University of Michigan College of Engineering- Manufacturing Engineering Course

Isn't it amazing when things work?

It is bemusing that I begin my statement of purpose with a tagline from our arch- rival, Honda. However, this statement is a symbol of Man's struggle, since ages, to understand every perceptible phenomenon, provide a scientific explanation to it, and craft his own unique influence on it.

I am a project engineer at Toyota's Indian operations, working for production engineering in the vehicle assembly shop. I want to be India's best lean operations consultant for companies intending to set up manufacturing operations in the Indian region.

With four years of learning experience at Toyota plants in three countries, I have wide experience in planning and implementing Toyota Production Systems. I specialize in the Vehicle Inspection Line and have built the surface inspection line and the function inspection line for Toyota India's new small car plant which became operational at the end of 2010. With a 150 million budget (in Japanese yen and Indian rupees) which I have handled independently, I have successfully met 5 milestones, from the first vehicle trial to the start of mass production.

I have worked for 16 months at Toyota Motor Corporation in Japan. At the Motomachi Plant in Toyota City, I have worked at the Global Production Centre, its training hub for creating global benchmarks in plant construction and operations. Trained in inspection equipment , I have also carried out equipment installation activities at Japanese plants with exclusively Japanese suppliers.

Working in the manufacturing sector has also made me grow as a person. Since the results are tangibly present for evaluation, the feedback for our work is much better, both qualitatively and quantitatively. Thus, the learning cycle with each product lifecycle is enhanced. Since it is impossible to hide any problem, we are forced to take up problems head- on and solve them.

I have completed my undergraduate degree at Bangalore's finest college for mechanical engineering. I have been fortunate to have found the company of high- achieving peers and the mentorship of distinguished faculty. My favorite subjects at college were operations research and automobile engineering. Hence, working for a company like Toyota was a natural aspiration, which later became a reality.

I also worked on an intensive project at Hindustan Aeronautical, India's leading aircraft maker at their Engine and Test Bed Research Centre. This project involved a material study and analysis to select a suitable alloy for the blades of the steam turbine of their upcoming commercial aircraft.

Apart from academics, I was actively involved in a variety of activities at college. I was a member of the college cricket team, as well as a founding member of the college quiz club and the mechanical engineering association. I have earlier played cricket at state- level tournaments for Bangalore City and also played league cricket. Since I was fortunate to have an urban- based, English- speaking background, I have helped the citizens of

Toyota City in Japan to converse in English as well as conducted citizen awareness programs for rural students of Toyota India's technical training institute near Bangalore.

At UMich, I wish to study towards a master's degree in manufacturing engineering. I believe that this course is a natural fit for me at this juncture in my career in operations as I will be able to effectively condense my four years of learning in the shopfloors of Toyota with a one- year focused study program in the same stream.

I intend to further strengthen my strong grasp of subjects like assembly & quality control, layout, process, and equipment planning with other aspects of manufacturing like advanced and non-traditional machining processes.

I find the curriculum offered in the manufacturing engineering course by UMich to be unique and one-of-it s- kind; of special interest are courses like global manufacturing, design for quality, and plant flow systems. These courses will provide me with the cutting- edge intellectual capacity required to be an effective operations professional.

There is also a natural convergence amidst my progression till now, my future career goals, and the Tauber Institute program. In order to be a successful lean consultant, I need to effectively integrate engineering and business perspectives, a thinking which is shared by the program and stated unequivocally in its mission. With my multi-country and multi-cultural work experience in project management, I am ideally suited to the program and can easily work on difficult projects with tight schedules, quality, and cost constraints.

Though I have a fixed plan, I intend to enter graduate school with an eager and open mind. I want to learn in a place where I am motivated, encouraged, and nurtured to be the best that I can be.

Living and working at Toyota City has already provided me with firsthand knowledge of how another culture approaches the tasks and challenges of everyday life. I am confident that a course at UMich will provide me with a more informed and accurate perspective of both business and engineering.

In the recent past, I have moved forward, the Toyota Way. I now request you, the admissions committee to provide me with a chance to move forward, the UMich Way.

Cover Letter
Strategic Planner Role at TVS Electric (Written in response to a specific job description)

Hello Mr.XX

A very good day to you.

It is my pleasure that I am being considered for the Strategic Planner role at TVS Motor's Electric Business. I feel that there is a significant overlap between my present work at Ola Electric & past firms and the requirements of this role. Hence, I have taken the liberty of providing a detailed Cover Letter in order to illustrate better the extent of this overlap.

As you are aware, I work with Ola Electric, one of India's leading Startups involved in making Electric Vehicles.

A fan of mobility and lately electric mobility, I believe that firms like Ola which operate fleets are in a great position to electrify their fleet. This is based from the simple logic that the Total Cost of Ownership model works amazingly well when the running cost of the vehicle is significantly higher than the Sticker Price, which is indeed the case with fleet- based vehicles which are utilized much more than vehicles for personal use. And, Swapping works really well for fleets starting from Auto Rickshaws as there is a proliferation of Auto Rickshaw Stands which could accommodate battery swapping stations.

However, we have to overcome multiple hurdles to get closer to the vehicle electrification goals which India and other countries have set for themselves. Customer adoption of a new form of usage, Range anxiety, and Standards Creation are just some of the most prominent ones. Firms and customers have to deal with multiple externalities in this EV journey and we still haven't answered a lot of questions about these externalities, which is why I perceive this role as interesting and important.

I will be picking up each of the responsibilities mentioned in the Job Description and elaborating on my relevant experience. My answers are in *Italics*. Please note that I will be actively striving to maintain the confidentiality required of my current position in my attempt to elaborate.

- Translating management vision, market dynamics, and consumer insights into Business Strategy & Planning.

I have created the Overall Company Roadmap for Ather. On a Business Level, I have worked on a target Valuation for Ather over a 10- year horizon derived as a product of the EBITDA numbers projected from different streams of businesses and Industry Multiples of Enterprise Value/ EBITDA for companies in similar spaces. The Revenues have been derived from our Secondary Market Research peppered with what we feel are the most likely scenarios. The costs are primarily internal projections.

- Developing product & technology roadmap by conducting market research and analysis. Organizational strategy & planning long- term strategy to meet shareholders' vision and short- term tactics.

I am working on two activities around the Product and Technology Roadmap. The first centers around getting inputs from leaders in these two areas about their vision of product and technology evolution.

The second activity, initiated just now is to create a Feature Value Attribute Analysis, where we analyz e the important features of all our products, collect data on either the perceived value to customers or a willingness to pay for them, and then map these back to the sub-systems of the product which enable these features. The total cost of providing these sub-systems (from design and development all the way until disposal) is being calculated and the ratio of value to cost will be analz sed to see if we are spending properly on features which are of value to customers. Additionally, we are building Market Intelligence Tools and Databases for our leaders.

- Exploring new business opportunities, evaluating and piloting them, and creating new businesses.

I am currently evaluating multiple business opportunities where we look at parameters like fitment to our roadmaps, NPV, Resource Requirement, and In-House Vs. Outsourcing options. Some of these opportunities are,
  - *Securing the Supply Chain for Cells made as per our requirement.*
  - *Business plans around Charging Infrastructure and Energy Storage.*
  - *Reducing Costs by consolidating the facilities we operate from by actively working with State Governments with Proposals to move all our facilities.*

- Exploring synergies with strategic partners and partnering with objective business goals.

I have worked at the back end to create Partnership models for some of the above business plans. However, in my previous stint at Cyient Limited, I have actively worked in this area by providing Synergy

Analysis and Business Development Support to a Firm we acquired and exploring multiple partnerships around Digital Manufacturing and 3D Printing.

- Gathering market intelligence, analyz ing competition, and keeping up with industry & consumer trends.

I have created a Market Intelligence tool which captures Media News, Profiles of Firms associated with Electric Vehicles, Industrial Policies from around the country and globally, and Product Specifications of Competitors. This is manually being updated today by our team members and we are working to automate it.

- Representing our vision and views at public and govt forums and working with them on industry policies.

I represent Ather at stakeholder meetings with the State Governments of Karnataka, Tamil Nadu, and Tela ngana and have deep connections with the Industries Department in these states. This is by virtue of working on proposals to set up Ather's new Manufacturing Facility (which we have eventually signed up with the Tamil Nadu Government) and conducting multiple rounds of negotiations around Subsidies that these Governments would offer us. I had provided feedback to the Draft EV Policies of these states (Tela ngana is yet to release, Tamil Nadu has released in November 2019 and Karnataka is amending it s Policy first released in 2017)

- Managing corporate communications and public relations

Haven't worked actively in this area.

- Evaluating potential investors and managing investor relationships.

Haven't worked actively in this area at Ather. However, in my stint at Cyient, I have been at the other end of the table, conducting Operations Due Diligence for 4 Target Companies that we evaluated before acquiring one of them.

Application Forms

In my opinion, application forms are the most time-consuming portion of an application and though efforts have been made in the last 5 years or so to scrape data that you upload through the resume and then parse it into various sections, we have to inevitably end up editing and modifying the content.

I have no great wisdom to impart on how to write great application forms as all they ask for are facts. Since this activity is unavoidable, let us think about the next best thing; minimizing the time we spend on it and not making glaring mistakes.

- Gather all your particulars from roughly high school onwards in an Excel table. All you have to do is Ctrl+C and Ctrl+V.
- Similarly, download all your documents to a central cloud location for a quick upload. I have a Google Drive folder which has all my documents ever since I was around 10 years old.
- Make sure that the documents you have uploaded are mandatorily optimized for both readability and file size. What typically happens is that upload has a size restriction and people have to resort to compressing files through public websites, which are not all that great on the confidentiality front.
- Invariably have version control on your key documents like resume. Just a mention of the date on which that particular version has been created is useful and avoids the chances of you sending an outdated version.
- As mentioned above, use any auto-fill software provided by the institution for which you are applying , but be sure to verify that the data is accurate. In my experience, the places where we

often tend to face problems are job titles, descriptions of work, and addresses.
- As much as possible, avoid writing long paragraphs directly on the application form's website. It is almost always easier to use Microsoft Word or Google Docs, edit repeatedly, and then paste the final version on the site.
- If you know the person who is going to look at the application, do follow up with them through either mail or phone on whether it is complete in all aspects.

Other Essays

Any essays apart from statements of purpose are usually sought during college applications and very seldom for job interviews. Usually accompanied by a word count limit, they seek specific replies from you and fortunately, come with a word count limit.

Within the space of around 600 words, which is equivalent to 3 to 6 paragraphs or 1 to 1.5 pages, you need to give your complete perspective on a narrow topic in the STAR framework.

Essays are daunting not because of the length of the submission required but because of the requirement to reflect deeply, and inwardly. Take the typical question of where you want to be 5 years from now on. How many people reflect on this on even an annual basis ? Hardly any that I know of, to be honest. In that sense, they are invaluable tools outside of the purview of application forms.

Coming back to our endeavor of creating effective essays, consider the below framework:

- 1 Paragraph: State one or two hypotheses that you hold true about the topic of the essay. This can be a short, 2- sentence or 3- sentence paragraph.
- 2-3 Paragraphs: Give detailed facts, opinions, and anecdotes in support of the hypotheses.
- 1 Paragraph (optional): Acknowledge the counter to your hypotheses with some brief facts and mention in what circumstance it would be valid. Reiterate why your hypotheses are better.
- 1 Paragraph: Conclude by reiterating that your hypotheses are held true because of the content stated above.

Some essay questions to practice with

- What book has influenced you deeply ?
- Who is the person you admire the most and why?
- Describe a significant incident that has changed your viewpoints in life.
- How will your area of specialization contribute to your long-term career plan?
- Describe your personal success and how it relates to your chosen field.
- Pick an experience in your life and explain how it has changed you.
- Describe your long-term perspectives for your long-term goals.
- Mention family or personal circumstances that have affected your financial status.

Interviews

> "*Trust yourself. You know more than you think you do.*"
>
> **– Dr. Benjamin Spock**

At no point of time in the whole process of admissions and job applications are you more tense than in the 5 minutes or so before the interview starts. And for good reason.

Interviews are obviously the place where you most prominently interact with a personality and not an email ID , a website, or even a voice on the phone. From the perspective of the candidate, that is both bad news and good news. Bad news, because with personalities come their biases, moods, and other baggage. Good news, because you can make at least these biases work in your favor with the help of some smart preparation .

Two mindset changes that I have adopted over the last few years have helped me make my peace with interviews.

a. The belief is that, as much as the candidate needs the admission or the job, the interviewer needs to fill up the seat or the job. This has given me the attitude to walk up to any interview room with the assurance that I am not in an inferior bargaining position and I believe possessing this attitude is like half the battle won.
b. My definition of success in an interview is as follows:- if you have steered the conversation towards the subjects you are most prepared with, and hence most confident of speaking about, and have thus satisfactorily answered any follow- up

queries that the interviewer may have, the interview is wildly successful. Consequently, if the interviewer, because of the limitation of time and the confidence that he/she has gained from talking to you does not go beyond what he/she has been steered towards, the chances of you not clearing the interview are extremely slim.

My discussion around this topic revolves around three or four stages of the interview.

24 hours to 1 week before the interview

- Common to all types of interviews
  - Make sure that all the documents that you have submitted have indeed reached the interview panel.
  - Prepare answers to a long list of questions which appear most often in interviews. A common pool of questions is listed at the end of this chapter for your reference.
  - Know your resume well enough to be able to speak about the points mentioned in it even when you are woken up in the middle of the night. In most cases, this is the one document which will mandatorily be read by the interview panel and they are likely to pick up any thread from anywhere in the resume that sparks their interest. It's akin to cold calling in many business school classes.
  - Take the help of trusted and skilled people to practice with 2 to 3 mock interviews before the big day. Importance should be given to their prior experience matching with the job or the admit, their closeness to you, and the candidness and detailing with which they give you feedback. Make sure that they particularly give feedback on body language, tone,

and filler words (um, ahh, like) and filler phrases (honestly speaking, if you ask me, it is my belief that). Also, make sure that at least one interview is a stress test where the interviewer deliberately makes the process uncomfortable by asking you such questions. Record the session and observe how you performed.

- Apart from preparing to answer questions about yourself and the course/role, there are a couple of types of questions that you need to practice answering. Some examples of both types are listed at the end of this chapter
  - Practice answering curveballs and guesstimate questions. Clarify the questions once more break them into small and easily estimable pieces, estimate with gross accuracy, and then aggregate again to conclude
  - Speaking impromptu on a random topic. Some questions that have cropped up in IIM interviews- " Do politicians distrust entreprenuers ? ", " Toilets are the new temples".
- If interviewing for an admit,
  - Understand all the courses available in the institute and how they will be useful to you. Make a shortlist of the 3 to 5 most relevant courses or areas as per you.
  - Research the history of the institute and some of the famous alumni who have studied there. If possible, try to reach out to at least 3 of them on their perspective of their biggest gains from attending the institute and the culture of the campus. Usually, the more recently the alumnus has attended this school, the better the perspectives.
- If interviewing for a job,
  - Talk to at least 3 current employees and maybe one employee who has recently left the firm about their opinions about the

company, the work, the team, and your reporting manager. Triangulation is a great way to reduce cognitive biases that any one individual might possess.
- Read and re-read the job description and then once more. Modify your resume, only subtly to make sure that all the major elements of your resume that match with the job description are indeed properly highlighted.
- If you are interviewing for a specific technology or skill and you already possess it,
  - make a long list of the projects that you have successfully completed or are currently involved in, using said technology or skill. It is great to portray the actual project itself if possible using digital media.
  - Also, it is useful to show projects that you have done beyond the scope of your actual work, either at your firm or outside. This is a very positive indicator of your intent to excel in that skill.
  - Be prepared to solve a real- life problem. It is better to go into the interview with a digital device like a tablet or a computer with pre-filled formats/ templates that help you solve the problem faster. You will definitely be appreciated for your initiative and fastidiousness !
- For most business- based (and even technology- based) roles, in case you are new or do not know a lot about the industry, do the following:-
  - Prepare (or if not possible, at least get hold of) a Porter's 5 Forces analysis and PESTLE analysis of the Industry, which is not more than a year old.
  - Encompassing all the major products and services that the company offers, gather a list of 3 to 5 major suppliers

of the firm and 3 to 5 major customers of the firm (in the case of B2B, that is). Search with keywords involving the firm and its suppliers/ customers together with any major news over the last 6 months.
- In the case of the company being a privately held one, where a large amount of public information is not available, the proper recourse available is usually the company's website, which lists its history, products and services, the key regions in which it operates and sometimes a brief profile of its management team.
- Additionally, it makes sense to create a filter of publicly available news of around 6 months origin which might give an insight into where the company is presently.
- If the company is publicly listed, you only have to worry about information overload ! My recommendation is to read, in the following order.
  - The company's Wikipedia page provides a ready summary of the most salient points that they wish you and the general public to be aware of.
  - The Company's Last 3 years annual report. This is scary because each of these reports is upwards of 200 pages . Hence, take a glance at only these sections for a comprehensive snapshot:-
- Management discussion and analysis for management's commentary on how the previous year went and what they expect the next year to be like.
- 3 Financial statements- Balance sheet, profit and loss, and Cash flow. It is okay to just understand what have been the major trends across revenues and expenditures over the past three years.

- Using a website called Screener, measure some of their key financial indicators and ratios with their top two competitors.
  - If the company is a startup (especially an early stage one), none of this information is bound to be available. The only solution is to insist with the hiring team that they schedule multiple interviews/ discussions with many people, leading up to final rounds with the decision maker and asking them the same questions to glean out any major discrepancies. Making decisions about the company and its prospects based on only one or two interviews is bound to be disastrous.
  - The softer aspects. I have used Glassdoor and would recommend Glassdoor/ Indeed/Linkedin to search for all the major features they offer like employee reviews, salary ranges, and interview experiences. Particularly, for any major red flags raised by employees with regards to hiring practices, ethical practices, target setting, performance reviews, and so on.

24 hours before the interview

- All heavy lifting activities are to be avoided .
  - Avoid making any last- minute changes to your documents, particularly if you have already submitted them to the concerned people.
  - There is no use brushing up on the details of that technology you profess to be an expert in, especially if you already have many many years of implementation experience .
- If possible, try to find out who exactly you will be interviewing with. Then, use publicly available information (absolutely

avoid stalking !) to obtain a good understanding of their personality. Does that person hail from the same city as you do ? Do you both have similar hobbies outside of work ? Any talking point that gives you either real or perceived benefit over other candidates must be actively sought and used.
- If you know of other candidates who are traveling at the same time to the same destination, it works to plan your schedules together.
- Make sure that you are logistically covered in terms of getting to the destination. If required to travel to a different location, make sure you travel the previous night.
- Get a great night's sleep, without worrying about the consequences of the interview process .

The interview

- I have next to zero credentials when it comes to fashion and clothing advice or opinions so let me keep this simple. Prioritize your clothing in the following order: based on how professional it looks, how comfortable you feel wearing it, and how convenient it is. The only other point I may add is to not shock anyone, particularly the interview panel with your looks. There is a very slim chance that you might stand out in a positive way.
- Taking a cue from my earlier reference about not imagining oneself as being in an inferior bargaining position, recalibrate yourself from the overwhelming that is surely bound to happen when you actually get into the interview location/ room and meet the people in person. Any kind of triggering could do. Maybe just a written sticky note that says that they need you as

much as you need their admit or offer. Or your resume, where you take a glance at all your past achievements. One advice that was given to me, and sounded plausible, was to stand in front of a full-length mirror with your hands on your hips for a few minutes. This is apparently found to increase your self esteem.

- The ultimate test in an interview, particularly in the case of say MBA interviews is to ignore all the noise around you in the last hour leading up to when you walk into the interview room. Consider the sources of the noise;
  - Any niggles in reaching up to the waiting area outside the interviewing room.
  - The aura around the campus where you are interviewing.
  - The confidence of the people around you going about their daily routines whereas you are tensed in waiting for a potential life-changing moment.
  - If interviewing as a batch, the personalities, attitudes, and conversations with other candidates. Someone who has worked all over the globe while you have never stepped foot outside of that plant in rural India. An IIT alumnus to your Tier-2 College. The candidate who didn't get selected last year and has re-appeared this year seems to know every single thing the interview panel will ask.
- There are multiple ways we can overcome the above factors. One simple and useful way is to actually visit the campus earlier if possible, or even the hotel ballroom/ conference hall where the interviews take place. In this case, familiarity breeds comfort and confidence . Another way is through mock interviews, which have been discussed earlier. Assume that you are exactly on the same playing field as every other candidate and that

selection will only be based on the interview's performance. More often than not, this is true as well!

During the interview

- Make every effort possible to steer the conversation towards the topics that you feel absolutely comfortable discussing. Even a simple leading question like *"Tell me about yourself"* should be used for the same purpose.
- However, it is also important to not meander towards absolutely irrelevant things. Crispness is also very appreciated.
- Practice interviews such that you avoid making an abnormal amount of body gestures. What happens is that the interviewers are more likely to remember you for your quirks rather than the answers you gave.
- As with resumes, make sure that you mention things that the interviewer is bound to remember you by. For example, you have worked in a country that very few people have been to. Or that you play a game at a highly competitive level.
- Asking a doubt when the question is not clear >>>> not asking the doubt, assuming wrong, and replying inappropriately.
- Saying *"I don't know"* to a question which you have no clue about >>>> trying to fake your way out with a reply.
- It is usually more important to be reasonably accurate with some speed than to be absolutely precise but takes a lot of time to come up with a reply.
- It is always great to take a few minutes to reply to a question that requires analysis. In such cases, it is highly advisable to

start jotting down your thought process on a piece of paper, all the while indicating clearly to the interview panel about the steps you are undertaking to solve the problem. More often than not, they are likely to help if they feel you are going drastically wrong.
- When provided a chance to ask any question about the firm, the one trick I found to have always worked is to ask the interviewers about themselves, their work in the organization, and their perception of its culture. This works for a very simple reason, everyone loves talking about themselves and is glad to find any such opportunity!
- Additionally on the above topic, refrain from asking a question whose answer can be found in the public domain. Ask something that only an insider will have a chance of knowing and might feel comfortable sharing.
- If presented with an offer during the interview itself, always ensure that you do not respond with an immediate answer. Always thank them for the offer and mention that you will give it your full consideration and revert within a reasonable and stipulated time. The reason for this is that the mindset that is required to decide upon an offer is not the same as the mindset that is required to perform optimally in the interview and it is absolutely impossible to switch between these two effectively.

After the interview

- You definitely score brownie points for sending the recruiter a thank you note for the opportunity to interview. It is even

better if you do not start following up on the results of the process at this juncture.
- If you have mentioned to anyone in the interview panel that you will share some additional information (maybe a link to the work you have done), do forward the same to them.
- I would absolutely recommend not to spend any time pondering over the results of the interview. What you know is only how you think you did. What you do not know is the criticality of the role, the interviewer's perception of your fitment, their assessment of your performance, the performance of other competing candidates, and so on. With this limited and insufficient information at your disposal, any analysis of your chances is a complete waste of time.
- Follow- up after 3 days, a week, and every subsequent week is, in my opinion, the right time frame. This is in case no reply is forthcoming from the hiring team. I would recommend at a maximum to have 3 follow- ups. In case there is no communication after these attempts, I believe that the opportunity is not worth pursuing further.

Sample List of Questions to Prepare for

It is preferable to write the answers to each of the questions in an Excel sheet

About you Questions
- Tell us about yourself.
- Tell us about the members of your family, where they stay, and their occupations.
- What are your hobbies?

- Why do you want to study at this institute/ work at this organization ?
- Describe your career till now in your own words.
- What is unique about you as a candidate ?
- Define success and failure in your words.
- Explain the gap in your resume/ change in your career path (if indeed applicable)
- How do you prioritize your work ?
- What is your perspective of how your supervisor/ manager should be like ?
- How do you think a former supervisor/ manager would describe you as ?
- Who are your role models and why ?
- What do you know about our organization ?
- Where do you want to be in 3 years/ 5 years ?
- Why did you stick to your previous organization for XX years ?
- Tell me something about yourself that is not in your resume.
- Is there anything else you would like for us to know ?

Questions to be answered using STAR framework

- Given a chance to pursue any other career, what would you be ?
- What did you most/ least enjoy about your previous work employment ?
- Give an example of a situation in which you provided a unique solution at work
- Give an example of a situation where you stood up to authority to do the right/ ethical thing.

- Give an example of a situation where you had to completely change the direction of the activity you were pursuing.
- Give an example of a time in which you worked under pressure.
- Give an example of your work in a team.
- What is a tough situation you have faced ?

Goofy/ Curveball questions

- Which animal would you compare yourself to and why ?
- What are the 3 uncomfortable questions that you would ask yourself ?
- What are 3 interesting things that you have done in life ?
- Sell me this pen/ book/ any other prop
- If given a chance to be/ meet any famous person from history, who would you want that to be and why ?
- Give us 3 reasons to not select you
- If you had the ability to go back in time and change something in your life, what would it be ?

Guesstimate questions

- Estimate the number of EV charging stations required for 2 Wheelers in Bangalore.
- Estimate the number of refrigerators sold in India every year.
- Estimate the number of Idlis/ Parathas made in India every morning.
- How many tennis balls can fit inside this room ?
- How many people live in your apartment complex ?
- How much water can fit into this room ?

Group Discussions

> "A good discussion increases the dimensions of everyone who takes part."
>
> – **Margaret Mead**

In the context of our conversation, the above quote is not wholly real. The objective of a group discussion is to assess a bunch of candidates in a setting often replicated in real life, i.e. in a team collaborating with multiple unique personalities.

The group discussion works well in this regard because of the fact that it is very hard to not show your true nature in such an uncontrolled setting. When you know the nature of the person you are interacting with, you can prepare for the interaction and perhaps wear a mask when required. When this is unknown, you stick to your true self.

Not that there's anything wrong with this for most people who fall within normal behavioral patterns when it comes to temperament, aggression, and articulation. In fact, there are many places where it is desirable for teams to have varying personalities.

Having established this, let us come up with a list of parameters that assessors look for in group discussions. I would submit the following in the same order:- listening skills, coherence of speech, articulation, learnability, an eye for details, and the ability to discuss topics both in some breadth and depth.

In this regard, here are some ways in which group discussions can be comfortably aced:

- It is essential to demonstrate that you are fully present in the room and completely absorbed in the discussion. In this context, making eye contact with anything which is a distraction should be avoided. Phones, accessories that take away your attention, even another candidate who is stunningly beautiful.
- Where you sit with respect to other candidates and how you sit also matters. I have found out that sitting to the center or immediate left of the center, from the perspective of the assessing panel is able to garner the most amount of eye contact from them, which is obviously the desired result. Also, someone who is sitting completely leaning on a chair, not cross- legged, and has hands visible on a table is more likely to portray confidence and positivity.
- At the beginning of the group discussion, make a note of the names of all the candidates, mark their relative seating position using a simple illustrative representation, and always address them by their names. This exhibits a high level of personableness and is very positively perceived, enhancing the goodwill that you will receive from the panel and the other candidates.
- Attempt to either be the first or last to speak out. This translates into an opening hypothesis or closing summary of the topic or problem statement opposed. These are likely to register most in the panel's minds.
- If speaking only in between, endeavor to say something diametrically opposite to the popular opinion so that people will appreciate that you have an alternate point of view.
- If you are doing neither of the above two topics and find yourself only agreeing with the opinions already exposed, the only way

you can stand out is to either provide more insight or more details. Be very clear in distinguishing between your opinion and summarizing what you think is the group's opinion.

- Be coachable. Often, when the assessors believe that the discussions are progressing nowhere, they come up with direct (and sometimes subtle) hints. There is no demerit in taking up the hint to change track in the discussion.
- As stated in other sections of this book, try and come up with around 3 points or 3 illustrations for or against any topic that you are discussing. This shows both crispness and thoroughness in your discussion.
- Very seldom is it okay in a group discussion to interrupt someone who is already speaking. I feel that the only scenario when it is acceptable is when another person is indulging in vulgarity, malice, or even hate speech. In every other case, wait for them to finish before you speak up.
- Absolutely avoid attacking anyone. You are discussing ideas and opinions, not individuals or personalities.
- It is very hard to sustainably defend extreme points of view. If you happen to come across such a topic with other candidates who are rubbing you off wrongly, try your best to find counterbalancing points both for and against the topic and then mention what you hold to be the right opinion.

UNDERSTANDING AN ADMIT

> *The most important thing we learn at school is the fact that the most important things can't be learned at school.*
>
> **– Haruki Murakami**

The feeling of having won that admit. Liberation from that job. First- time travel to another country. The chance to study on really cool campuses. The admiration from close family and friends. Just the flight abroad. The fancy salary you will earn later.

These are but some of the few reasons why an admit should be celebrated.

However, with multiple admits comes the burden of having to choose the one school that you will call your own. You will have to make decisions under some level of uncertainty about the future as well as even impartial facts about the present.

In order to help frame this situation better, I submit that the process of understanding an admit be split into two things; understanding the choice of schools and understanding the programs themselves.

Understanding the choice of schools:- Rankings, cost of living, finance, brand equity, and network.

Understanding the choice of programs:- Length and mode of study, Faculty and research group, courses (core courses and electives), Faculty and research groups, alumni, and job prospects.

The undercurrent to your choices of schools, programs, and even countries of study is your appetite for risk and your forecast for the future. Are you risk- taking or risk- averse ? Do you have an optimistic, neutral, or pessimistic view of how the future looks like for the world as well as for you ? Are you okay with completely shifting from whatever you have pursued till now to pursue something else more lucrative ?

Selecting a school
Rankings

For a comprehensive listing of all known rankings of universities, please refer to the Wikipedia link here. Take your pick of the region, your familiarity with the agency conducting the ranking survey, and the size of the survey. For the sake of thoroughness, refer to a minimum of 2 different listings.

Personally, I am agnostic to the whole process and have not used rankings at any time when I was mulling over admissions. Though colleges trumpet any improvement in rankings and candidates quote them as major factors for their choice, I think that rankings have limited utility. Apart from Boasting rights. University of Michigan, Ann Arbor is ranked #2 in 2023 in the US News Ranking for the Course I pursued, Manufacturing Engineering. IIM Ahmedabad is ranked #1 in 2023 in the Indian Government's NIRF rankings. There, I showed off. By the way, I used the rankings which showed these institutes in the best light possible !

When agencies compile rankings, I believe they are working on the basis of certain principles (note that I do not use the word motives or biases) that are not useful to you. Among the most important of these principles is to maintain the relevance of the ranking itself. That diminishes if every year, the same colleges occupy the same ranks.

Nobody would be interested in the 2023 rankings if they were the same as the 2022 edition, the 2021 edition, and so on. This, in my opinion, is incentive enough for the agencies to keep churning the list even when it's not really necessary.

Additionally, rankings have helped the top academic institutes to accumulate a sense of elitism and snobbery which at least partially converts into over-the-top fee structures for about the same quality of education and opportunities. Be mindful of this when you are comparing tuition fees later.

This is all the more muddled up by the fact that a tiny number of these institutions actively try to game the system, some couldn't care less and others altogether skip the activity. What this all adds up to is my surmise that rankings have limited utility in your mind space when choosing a place.

If you still want to somehow use rankings as part of your decision process, I recommend the following:

- As mentioned above, look at more than one ranking list and work with an average of rankings rather than with a single reference.
- Use rankings on a very gross basis. To illustrate, to choose a School with Rank #3 above a school with Rank #4 just for the sake of ranking should not be appropriate but to choose that school over another school with Rank #14 should be appropriate. My theory is that any school in the Top 10 ranks will fulfill all hygiene factors required for a wholesome experience, the next 10 ranks will have this a notch lower, and so on.
- Usually, the schools ranked in the Top 10 are known to everyone. The rankings might be more useful to you when your profile is more suitable to the schools placed in the next 10 ranks and so on.

- Ideally, rankings should be used when you have more than 3 admits, to filter the number down to 2 or 3. The remaining 2 or 3 being roughly placed in the same vicinity in terms of rankings, a host of other parameters discussed in this chapter should be used to select the one.
- Another good way of using rankings is as a well-organized database with information that is otherwise hard and time-consuming to accumulate.
- Ensure that the time frames of different rankings you are choosing are the same and if not, adjust for them. A lot of surveys might be collected from alumni who passed out last year and you will be graduating from the course 1 or 2 years later. This already results in a 2-year time gap because of which a whole bunch of data points might have completely changed. Something from 2 to 3 years ago may or may not hold true.
- Look for some major trends over the years and if they matter to you. Diversity. The average salary in a certain sector. Faculty's research output. The percentage of international faculty.
- Pay closer attention to the further categorization of rankings of an institute only if it has fallen more than 10 ranks over a period of 5 years or so. If the root cause is a parameter that is not of much importance to you, this too should be ignored.

Cost of Living

Apart from the tuition fee, a big chunk of money will be spent on daily expenses. There are a host of websites, including university-listed ones which give you a very specific range in terms of how much you may incur.

Some links for your reference:

https://www.universityliving.com/cost-of-living-calculator/journey - a reference to schools located in the UK, Australia, Canada, Ireland, and the US.

https://livingcost.org/cost - comparing cities globally.

Cutting across all the cost headings listed below, my standard advice after having lived abroad for work and education is this; prioritize your choices in terms of safety, quality, and then cost effectiveness. Particularly in a location which you have never been to before.

Another filter I have used to good effect when living abroad is to have my living situations sorted to a level of comfort such that they do not become a distraction to my primary objective. Hence, do not pinch money to live in housing much beyond the campus when it requires you to spend hours on the road, hours which could have been better spent on your studies. Same for preparing food.

I have had a dangerous experience in the US where a robbery took place from my student accommodation in Ann Arbor, Michigan when I was sleeping in the same room. Thankfully, the only loss was my wallet and some money swiped through a debit card. Given that my apartment was in a secluded part of the university and I happened to stay alone at that time (as my allocated room mate canceled his admission at the very last minute), I very promptly switched over to housing in the center of the town for the next term and housed with friends of mine.

The major expenses that you should account for (taking the extreme case of staying abroad) are housing, food, transportation, daily miscellaneous expenses, entertainment, a few fun trips, traveling for interviews and seminars, and trips back home.

A good thumb rule I have used to budget for expenses (which carries on much beyond my student years) is to figure out the amounts under each of the above heads, consolidate them into a range, add in a 20% buffer to the maximum amount in the range for extraordinary situations and use this sum to arrange for funds, either through your own or through education loans.

Of course, keep a monthly tab on each of these, stay frugal, and endeavor to stay close to the minimum amount you had projected and you will not need to utilize the full extent of the credit, which helps you breathe easier when it is time to start paying back.

The good part about living as a student is that you do not need to show off your wealth (or the lack of it) and through your circle of peers, you have an endless supply of cost-cutting ideas available to you to either consider or ignore.

It is but natural that the first two months will be more expensive as you are still getting your banking mechanisms up, and exploring different options while you get settled in. It is better to keep more physical cash with you for this time period.

Finance

On the education economics front, Let us keep domestic spending apart and talk about the elephant in the room, the money spent abroad. The latest figures are $80 Bn in foreign exchange sent abroad for the 11 lakh students who went in the last year. Interestingly, this wipes out most of the foreign exchange that we get from NRI remittances.

On a per capita basis, this translates into a spend of Rs. 60 Lakhs. One survey I have seen defines the Middle Class in India as earning between 5 lakhs and 30 lakhs annually. This 60 lakh amount is then twice the annual salary of the richest households in this bracket. It is the universal truth in India, with very few exceptions that parents save for and then spend on their children's education. Simply put, education abroad of even a single child wipes out almost all the savings of many households.

My mother worked for a PSU bank where she spent many years providing education loans to candidates to pursue courses across the world. Consequently, I have heard of the Good, the Bad, and the Ugly when it comes to financing education.

In the entire span of your career, the greatest gift you can give to your parents is this. Make sure that your foreign education dreams do not wipe out their savings. Do whatever you want in this regard. Defer education plans for a couple of years. Choose colleges where you have confirmed scholarships. Make sure that you are not choosing a college only for its snob value. Finish your courses at a much faster pace than any other students would if the school allows this and cut your education expenses by half (I did this at Michigan).

From a financial perspective, you are much better off if you plan to earn in the same currency that you are spending on your education. The only other exception to this situation would be if you are loaded with money, don't need a loan in the first place, and can write off the complete amount as a learning experience and nothing else. Try to factor in job opportunities for your specific sector and skills.

Understanding an Admit

On financing for domestic education, most of the large Indian banks offer partial and full education loans at very competitive interest rates, sometimes with no collateral if the admission is to an elite institution. For example, check out SBI's website for a comprehensive list of the different schemes available for education funding. Even here, a combination of mostly education loans and partial savings should help with an exploration of further funding opportunities.

On the last topic, I encourage admitted candidates to pursue all manners of funding opportunities through scholarships. All it costs is the time taken to write an email or submit an application. The upside is funding if granted and also the chance to participate in a competitive process and there is absolutely no downside. Lists like the one attached here should help you narrow down relevant scholarships.

What about working part-time, particularly for students working abroad ? From what I have seen in universities abroad, roughly half the students who work part-time do so in jobs which are academically oriented (like teaching or research assistantship) and the other half take up anything available. I strongly believe that the former will be beneficial and the latter should be avoided if possible.

If you think that you have an extra 20 hours every week, I would recommend that you rather negotiate with the office that manages your program to ensure that you finish the program one or two terms earlier by cramming up more credits in every term. Any full-time job that you are able to get earlier is certain to pay more than your hourly wages gained by working part-time and add more relevant work experience to your resume.

Since this is money we are talking about and it is easily quantifiable, let us attempt to show financing discussions in a table. In order to do so, a small introduction to a couple of topics.

a. Opportunity cost:- If you had the option of
   o Studying for two years and
   o Working with a salary of Rs. 10 lakhs per year for two years the opportunity cost would be Rs. 10 lakhs x 2= Rs. 20 lakhs
b. Sunk cost:- If you have already paid Rs. 20 lakhs for a 2-year course, have finished 1 year already, and are confused about whether the course is going to add any value and whether you should study further, the 20 lakhs is a sunk cost. It has happened in the past and you cannot redeem it back no matter what.
c. Net present value:- If you earn Rs. 10 lakhs today and earn Rs. 11 lakhs one year from now, with the bank interest rate at 10%, the net present value of your total earnings
   Rs. 10 Lakhs + [Rs. 11 Lakhs/ (1+10%)]
   = Rs. 10Lakhs + [Rs. 10 Lakhs]=Rs. 20 Lakhs.

Based on the above, for all the different choices you have, prepare tables like the two examples shown below. Cash inflow is shown as positive and cash outflow is,

Understanding an Admit

Option 1:- Studying in India with loan-1 year MBA, working in India post MBA- NPV Rs. 38.5 Lakhs

1. 1 year MBA, all inclusive at 40 Lakhs
2. Loan repayment rate- Rs. 8.15%, 10 years repayment with loan to start after graduation

Assumptions Made		Year					
		0	1	2	3	4	5
Course Fees & Living Expenses	Rs. 40 Lakh total loan, with 10 year repayment at 8.15% interest, payable after graduation			-₹586,188	-₹586,188	-₹586,188	-₹586,188
Living Expenses post MBA	Starting at Rs. 1 Lakh per month Annual Inflation at 10%			-₹1,200,000	-₹1,320,000	-₹1,452,000	-₹1,597,200
Income	Base salary of Rs. 35 Lakhs with 10% increase every year		0	₹3,300,000	₹3,300,000	₹3,300,000	₹3,300,000
Cash Flow			0	₹1,513,812	₹1,393,812	₹1,261,812	₹1,116,612
Present Value	10%	₹3,853,439	0	₹1,251,084	₹1,047,192	₹861,835	₹693,328

Option 2:- Studying in UK with loan -21 month MBA, working in UK post MBA- NPV Rs 79.7 Lakhs

1. 2 1 month MBA, all inclusive at 110 Lakhs
2. Loan repayment rate- Rs. 8.15%, 10 years repayment with loan to start after graduation

	Assumptions Made	Year					
		0	1	2	3	4	5
Course Fees and Living Expenses	Rs. 110 Lakh total loan, with 10 year repayment at 8.15% interest, payable after graduation				-₹1,608,000	-₹1,608,000	-₹1,608,000
Living Expenses post MBA	Starting at 2000 GBP per month Inflation at 10%				-₹2,520,000	-₹2,772,000	-₹3,049,200
Income	Starting salary of 75k pounds (Base salary) with 5% increase every year		0	₹0	₹7,875,000	₹8,268,750	₹8,682,188
Cash Flow			0	₹0	₹3,747,000	₹3,888,750	₹4,024,988
Present Value	10%	₹7,970,446	0	₹0	₹2,815,177	₹2,656,069	₹2,499,201

Some pointers to make this table and the comparison more robust.

- Make sure that you are calculating all the options in the same currency. Preferably do it in the currency in which you are going to take a loan.
- The examples you see here are certainties. They have to incorporate probabilistic calculations. Take the examples below:
  ○ You are studying in India. After this, there is a 20% chance that you will get placed abroad with an average take-home salary of say 80,000 GBP (for the UK), which translates to Rs. 84.15 Lakhs, and a 80% chance that you will get placed in India with an average take-home salary of Rs. 35 lakhs. In this case, your take-home salary is ((84.15 x 20%) + (35 x 80%)), which is Rs. 44.83 lakhs.
  ○ Similarly, calculate the same for the option of studying abroad. There may only be a 50% chance of you being able to get a work visa and hence a job in the UK post your MBA and this should be well incorporated in your model.
- Use more details from the university fees and financing pages as well as resources available on cost of living in different cities. In most countries (and nowadays, increasingly in India also), the city in which you live and work determines your cost of living.
- As highlighted above in other places, always be conservative in your arrangement of funds by planning for the highest in the cost range.
- Add in separate rows for items like foreign exchange rate, increase in cost of living, and increase in salary in order to be able to fine-tune your model.

- Even if you have the money and do not need to take a loan, it might make sense to take an education loan as the cash outflow would start at a later point of time. This is assuming you believe you can get higher investment returns than the rate of the education loan.
- You can stretch the calculation up to the full extent of the loan term but the point is that latter years have lesser importance in the NPV model. This rightly incorporates the mindset that events much later in the future are less certain, less important, and hence should have lower weightage.

Brand equity

Which school you went to matters in your career and life, for sure. With the added application of what is popularly referred to as the Law of Diminishing Returns. If you go to IIM Ahmedabad at the age of 22 for a 2- Year MBA, it is much better than going to the same school at the age of 30 for a 1- Year MBA.

From my experience, and that of many people around me, my impressions about the utility of your school's brand are its ability to open doors and raise ceilings.

Your status as an alumnus of a good school will raise your chances of important people responding to you when you reach out to them for say, appearing as a guest at an event you are organizing . The response might be a yes, a no or a maybe but at least you get one, as compared to say some non- alumnus who might be completely ignored. And, if you are reaching out to a fellow alum, the response will have a notch higher level of sincerity.

Similarly, at whichever organization you belong to, you have a greater chance of being invited to join in discussions where important decisions are taken and would be provided with an opportunity to contribute. An invite and an opportunity that would otherwise take a non-alumnus many years of experience to obtain.

Over the course of your long careers, a collection of small interventions like the above two cases that I mentioned tend to certainly give you a higher than the above chance of succeeding wildly in your career and are the reason that people yearn to acquire the alumni status of prestigious schools.

Of course, it is needless to say that has to necessarily be accompanied by a high degree of conscientiousness, hard work, leadership abilities, and business acumen aptly and frequently demonstrated by actual results.

Additionally, if you have studied in a school with high pedigree or very high rankings, your probationary period tends to be very short and all eyes will be on you to start delivering results as soon as you hit the workforce. Indeed, with great entitlement comes great expectations.

There are apparently other benefits as well. Student and alumni discounts on popular sites, and exclusive credit cards. With reference to IIMIITMatrimony.com , I have nothing further to say on this topic.

This has to necessarily be a two-way street. On the cusp of our graduation, one of my MBA professors mentioned that we should benefit from the School's reputation for the first 5 years of our careers and then, for the rest of our lives, School should benefit from our reputation.

How do we objectively measure this parameter ? Rankings are one way but may not be the most relevant to you directly. I would recommend you do the following. If you have a list of between 3 to 5 schools that you are considering, send the list to around 10 people you know who have either studied at these schools, taught there, or have recruited from there and ask them to rank these schools by reputation.

Particularly, if recruiters tend to have a very favorable opinion about a school, the chances that they will visit this school for recruitment in even lean years is high, and this augurs well for your future prospects here.

By factoring in the bias of alumni, current students, and teachers and coming up with a weighted average rank, you should have a better sense of what a larger sample size perceives the reputation of each school to be like.

Network

When we hear the name network, one of the first things that comes to mind is a spider's web. Using this analogy, let me lay out a hierarchy that is useful for considering your perception of what a School- based network would be.

Classmates >>> Teachers>> Alumni >> Rest of the world.

Your classmates, particularly the few among them who comprise your study circles, bear the greatest influence on your learning experience in school, even more than what teachers bear. Particularly if many of these classmates themselves have come in with some diverse experience. More about teachers and Professors in our section on choosing a program

Hence, when you think about the network that you are getting from a course, what you are really considering is the diversity of your classmates. It is diversity in careers, in the geographic region from which they hail, and even what they aspire to be. Look for overall class profiles over the last 3 years or so to determine whether the course caters to the diversity you aspire to soak in.

The next indication of the strength of networking of a school can be found by taking a look at last year's calendar of key events where there was active participation of notable people from industry and academia. Often, the schools might be successful in pulling in alumni for such events but do even non-alumni participate and broadcast about their participation ?

The place where the campus is located is another key factor to consider. I studied Manufacturing Engineering in Ann Arbor, Michigan, and definitely benefited from the fact that the university is located near where the Auto Giants Ford, General Motors, and Chrysler are located. We often had very senior leaders from these firms, often alumni themselves come in to teach us as adjunct faculty and the vicinity was conducive to multiple automotive-centric learning experiences.

Similarly, if you aspire to a career in the IT sector and have an admit from both IIM Bangalore and IIM Lucknow, IIM Bangalore would easily make more sense considering the number of IT giants that have their presence in that city.

Selecting a School- Decision Matrix

Once you have all the above considerations comprehensively covered, a decision matrix shown in the below table can be quickly filled up.

- Financing and cost of living can be separate topics or the same larger topic of financial impact, depending on how you feel about the subject.
- The weightage shown below can be indicative and you can suitably modify them as per your perspective. For example, you may already have the money available and may give financing

a lesser weightage so that other parameters can be given more importance to.
- Use the second row in each parameter to fill up salient notes as a ready reckoner.
- Be very wary when you give scores in the extremes.
- When you see overall scores in the extremes, recheck to make sure that they are scored right. Maybe your gut instinct has already indicated you towards them. Post this, If you see a very low score, the option should be discarded and if you see a single very high score, the option must be considered above all.
- It is unlikely that the above is going to be the case and more often than not, you will be left with two out of the shortlisted options closely vying with each other for the top score and you need to take a judgment call on one of them.

Admits and Offers

Parameter	Weightage of Parameter (Adding to 100%)	Scale of 1 to 10, 10 is better			
		School 1	School 2	School 3	School 4
Network	20%	1	6	7	4
Brand Equity	20%	4	4	8	1
Financing	20%	9	9	7	7
Cost of Living	20%	4	2	8	6
Ranking	20%	8	1	6	5
	100%	**5.2**	**4.4**	**7.2**	**4.6**

Selecting a Program
Length and mode of study

- Length of study
    - Most academic programs at the post- graduate Master's level can take from as short as one year to as long as 4 years to complete . Doctoral studies can take from 2 years to 7 years. Most people on average complete Master's degrees in 1.5-2 years and PhDs in 3 -4 years.
    - The above indication of average time for completion is location- centric. Make sure to have an informal survey done through the program alumni website and linkedI n of how long people take to finish.
    - When researching programs, validate if the length of the program can be flexible based on your aptitude and appetite. It is always better to stretch and finish faster as you avoid getting bored with the course as well as get a chance to start earning earlier.
    - The above statement is particularly true for students who are going into courses with 2 or more years of experience. They are too accustomed to monthly salaries, can grasp concepts faster, and will get bored faster with longer terms of study.
    - Many students that I know of have taken up research assistantships to sustain their student visas and continue being on campus as they waited for the job environment to improve and to get a suitable job. This makes sense if you are clear that you will stay in the same country for the foreseeable future for your career but needs to be included in your finances.
- Mode of study

- With the advent of digital tools in education, you have a multitude of choices: full- time in campus, weekends on campus, distant learning with periodic visits to the campus, and even fully online.
- A preference for one of the above is based on financial ability, career alignment at work, and also the extent to which your current workplace supports study programs. I have worked across firms which lie on extreme ends of the spectrum with respect to the level of support that they provide to employees and fully acknowledge the rationale for every mode of study that people would pursue.
- I would always recommend full- time study on campus because the learning is amplified by the environment and the peer group. Every other mode of study will definitely provide various levels of diluted learning. As much as classrooms help, unstructured learning is even more critical. Additionally, it is mostly the case that job prospects are best accessed by full- time, on-campus candidates.
- If you are doing any mode other than full-time on-campus, be prepared to sacrifice your sleep for the duration of the course.
* Sabbatical/ Quit college and study ?
  - If you are seeking only learning, are reasonably content with your current firm, and have come across a lot of alumni from the same school in your firm who are faring well, it would be better to seek a sabbatical and funding from the firm.
  - The only caveat from the above is the kind of agreement that you sign with the firm for the same (to serve for 3-5 years post- study with the firm in lieu of a penalty) and whether

you are comfortable to stick with the current firm without regret for this time frame. I would refrain from signing such an agreement with the twisted belief that it can be broken later with only monetary implications; the loss of trust and goodwill will come back to bite you for sure .
- In every other scenario, it is better to quit your current job and pursue full- time study and then pursue career opportunities through school. Anyway, financing is usually not a concern and loans are usually available at reasonable rates and sometimes without any collateral for premium institutes.

Core Courses and Electives

- Core courses should give you breadth and the electives should give you a combination of breadth and depth.
- If you are doing a technical course,
  - English is the medium of instruction. If you know the teachers who are teaching, check out their videos on Youtube to see if you understand their accents.
  - You are taught some elements of research methods and data analytics.
  - Almost everyone is building multiple prototypes and some of them have even taken their projects into commercialization.
  - People from industry and research are coming in and teaching at least 20% of the time (predominantly in electives) .
  - Make sure that you have between 20-30% in a business setting. In this context, going to a university which also

has a business school has huge benefits because chances of interaction with industry leaders are very high.
- If you are doing a business course
    o The bedrock of the program is a General Management focus. I believe that the foremost qualification of a business course is to teach the students to become general managers, able to cut across functions and departments that they are aligned with and think about the larger good of the company.
    o The learning pedagogy is heavily biased towards case study learning, where study groups comprised of diverse students prepare and submit for a case where they assume the role of a protagonist and discuss the same in class.
    o Immersive learning experience- Comprised of experiential learning projects, international trips, and simulations- based business games where much of the learning can be applied. They usually start after core courses end.
    o If you are doing a specialization, understand if you can pivot by the time the core courses end. Your interests might change during the course of your classes and you should not be locked into a specialization without the chance to explore outside
    o Professors of practice/ adjunct faculty teach at least 20% of the course.
    o I have felt that Grade non- disclosure is better for the entire class as it fosters positive competition, particularly for a classroom where the average work experience is more than 4 years or so.

Faculty and Research Group

- In every university, Faculties do many roles like teachers, researchers, administrators, consultants, and even marketers for the school. The role that is most critical and relevant for you is as a teacher, closely followed by a researcher. Make sure to go through videos of the faculty in the classroom to check if their body language as a teacher impresses you.
- The reputation of the faculty, as determined by sites like Ratemyprofessors. Though there is a chance of malicious students disproportionately staggering the ratings, I believe there are enough ratings to average out such instances.
- Their research prowess and fame, as indicated by popular metrics like the h-index.
- The infrastructure available in the research (and to a lesser extent, the classroom) facilities. I believe this is certainly a place where some of our Indian universities lag behind their counterparts in other countries. I know of a friend who took much longer to finish his course simply because there was no staff available in the laboratories for mundane activities and hence he had to do every single chore .
- If at all possible, and without being creepy, try to glean information about your potential research colleagues. It is my understanding that you spend more hours with them than with classmates with whom you do coursework or with the faculty themselves with whom there is unlikely to be daily interaction.
- Have any students dropped out of the program ? If so, understand the reasons why they have dropped out.

Alumni

- Have the alumni also made a mark for themselves as working professionals or as academics ? This is an indication of the quality of the faculty, the group, and the program.
- Are the alumni willing to provide precise feedback about the program and if so, is it favorable ?
- Will the network be a source of support when you graduate ?

Jobs

- Statistics speak for themselves. In the last 3 to 5 years, what percentage of the program has been placed? Are there attributable reasons as to why some of the students have not been placed and has there been a concerted effort by the program to improve in these areas over the years ?
- Where the alumni have landed can be a powerful but not conclusive indicator of where you might be headed. It is also useful to understand if what they are presently doing motivates you sufficiently to pursue whatever course you are on .
- Understand the level of industry interaction, through faculty consulting assignments, distinguished speaker sessions, and most importantly student projects sponsored by the industry.
- Are there enough networking opportunities available at regular intervals specifically through career fairs ? Are these being promoted and driven by alumni who work for different firms ?

Selecting a Program- Decision Matrix

Parameter	Weightage of Parameter (Adding up to 100%)	Scale of 1 to 10, 10 is better			
		School 1 Program 1	School 1 Program 2	School 2 Program 1	School 2 Program 2
Length & mode of study	20%	5	6	6	9
Core Courses and electives	20%	3	10	7	1
Faculty and research Groups	20%	8	2	4	9
Alumni	15%	10	5	8	4
Jobs	25%	6	4	3	9
	100%	**6.2**	**5.35**	**5.35**	**6.65**

NEGOTIATING AND SELECTING AN OFFER

The principles of negotiation

During my final term at the IIMA- PGPX program in 2016-17, my friends Akshay, Vinit and I had written a paper is part of our course submission for the Negotiations Lab Course and has been perceived by the authors to serve as both a reflection piece based on their experiences as well as a helpful document for future PGPX candidates on the job market. I believe that this paper, with suitable modifications, is still suitable for this segment of the book. Though this is MBA- centric, it can be ubiquitous for negotiations across all types of roles

The framework of the paper rests on the 15 rules of negotiating a job offer which has been laid out by Prof. Deepak Malhotra

(HBS) in a Harvard Business Review Article. However, instead of relying on the content of the article, we discussed the application of these rules in their localized context of the negotiation of job offers for their batchmates. All attempts had been made to generalize learning. Many thanks to Akshay and Vinit for letting me use this piece here and also to Prof Biju Varkkey, an awesome teacher.

Methodology

In the process of preparing for the recruitment process at PGPX, the authors of this paper saw a video on the 15 rules for negotiating job offers by Prof. Deepak Malhotra of the Harvard Business School. We found these rules useful and relevant to our subsequent experiences both as candidates in the job market and as members of the placement committee (one of the authors). Hence, we propose to add our interpretation to each of the 15 rules and also cite practical experiences about these rules.

Link to the Original HBR article: https://hbr.org/2014/04/15-rules-for-negotiating-a-job-offer

YouTube: https://youtu.be/km2Hd_xgo9Q

Link to the book Negotiations Genius: http://amzn.in/5K0dHXA

1. **Don't underestimate the importance of likeability**

We feel that a good way to internalize this aspect is to religiously follow one of the cardinal rules of a consulting career, which is "Don't be an asshole." Many roles in consulting and other client-facing scenarios (which are the norm in post-MBA jobs) place much emphasis on the impression the candidate creates as the company is evaluating whether they can confidently place the candidate in front of their clients. Even when a candidate has a point of contention that he/she feels is significant, the way in which it is put across needs to come across as professional and dignified.

First impressions are crucial, and the way a job offer is being negotiated provides insight into the character of both the candidate and the company. In many cases, we have seen that the candidate is not willing to go ahead with roles where he is not impressed by the recruiter, owing to some reasons like the recruiter not being prepared, being rude, or stalling the candidate for time unnecessarily.

2. **Help them understand why you deserve what you are requesting**

We have been witness to many discussions involving the choice of location or function where the candidate can articulate why he/she would choose one option over another. This is particularly important in the context of programs like the one- year MBA where many candidates are interested in switching functions or industries.

In such a case, it is not always easy to ask for a particular role as well as demand a certain seniority or a higher salary unless the candidate can justify the claims. If the firm is an established company with a traditionally strong hiring process with policies, they are not indulging in value discovery during the interaction with the candidate but instead have an excellent idea of what they should be offering. Hence, any delta in requirements is difficult to substantiate even for the recruiters within their organization.

3. Make it clear they can get you

When the candidate wants a particular job, and the negotiations are still in a zone of uncertainty, it is advisable to take a position that he/she is indeed keenly interested in the job but has a concern which will not be a roadblock, as a location constraint. Some candidates have shown agreement to sign on the spot if given an offer, perhaps showing too many of their cards! However, some positions that could be problematic and an awkward corner to get out of are:

a) The candidate is giving a hint that he/she is still evaluating the company and asks questions like why the company has fired some employees in the last quarter.
b) The company is interested in hiring the candidate for a particular role but does not have an opening at that point in time. However, the company wants to park the candidate in another position for a short period and move him/her later on. The candidate wants a particular function and is not open to any other choice.
c) The candidate asks the company what value they see in him. Unless the candidate is sure about how he/she will add value to the company and the role, it is not possible to portray clarity of why there is a fitment.

4. Understand the person across the table

It is critical for the candidate to research not only the company but also the representative. The candidate needs to understand the agent's position and role within the organizational structure of the company and accordingly carry out the conversations. For example, if the CEO is conducting the negotiations, there is a larger zone of possible agreement as the CEO can probably take a wider spectrum of decisions. An HR recruiter who is just coordinating for the duration of the interview process may not have such latitude and will have to convey every request back to the power centers within the organization.

One of the authors of this paper was guilty of following up incessantly with an employee of the hiring company on joining location and date, only to get to know in the third interaction that the particular employee was only responsible for entering the place and time preferences in the company's HR database and nothing else.

5. Understand their constraints

It is strongly advisable to approach a company and its representative as a party across the table and not an all-powerful patron whose every statement needs to be adhered to without question (of course, without being guilty of tilting too much towards the other extreme !). The company also has restrictions in its basket of negotiation options. For example, they need to recruit a minimum or a maximum number of candidates across different campuses.

No matter how much they like a candidate, companies cannot offer him/her more than a maximum range because of internal disparity. When a company hires more than one candidate, then agreement of higher compensation to one candidate would mean offering similar terms to all the other selected candidates.

6. Be prepared for tough questions

A blanket advice which applies to all situations is to never lie in a negotiation as it inevitably does long- term harm to the candidate. Even an iota of doubt about honesty and integrity will impact the candidate badly, especially in the context of the new relationship which is being built between the candidate and the company. Some tough questions that are usually encountered are:

a) Frequent job changes are difficult to answer.
b) A candidate needs to be very well prepared and show some relevance for switching functions.
c) The company might like to know if they are the top/only choice and may test this aspect by providing a spot offer and imploring the candidate to accept the offer immediately.
d) A current offer like a sabbatical should be pre-disclosed.

7. Focus on the questioner's intent, not on the questions

The underlying philosophy of this point is to understand that the topics raised by the company are not all fact seeking but may also be exploratory about the candidates and their frame of mind. For example,

a) The candidate is repeatedly asked if he/she is going to stay in the company. Often, offers are structured to lock in the candidate over a longer period. Some examples are a very low starting salary which escalates steeply after the candidate has

a proven track record over a period of two or three years or substantial stock options.
b) The candidate may be asked questions about previous compensation structures, and this discussion often has a broad range of probable implications. The range of salaries which the company might offer might not be aligned to the previous salaries.
c) The candidate needs to reassure the company in case of a movement from a bigger brand to a smaller brand.

8. Consider the whole deal

It is common for someone faced with a 15-minute discussion on the benefits to focus on a few points, especially salary and a key constraint such as location or employee band. It would be wise for a candidate to consider beforehand their requirements regarding the key and non-key criteria, and prioritize the same. Further, in the job description as well as the negotiation, a view must be obtained of both, the current offer and its near-term prospects.

If in a discussion, few of the parameters fit in well, and others are around the minimum levels set by the participant, the offer must be considered favorably, if the near-term prospects seek to improve on the key criteria further. An example can be where the candidate focused more on aspects such as immediate salary, and ignored the benefits such as leaves and paid international travel for family members, as well as the power of the position offered.

In another case during the year, we have observed a few people ignore a few offers due to lack of immediate salary benefits ostensibly to offset the repayment of the education loan while being completely aware of the dominant position it would have thrust them into in a short span of time. An easy- to- observe case could be "leadership programs". Essentially, it is not important to optimize on every parameter and see which other parameters can compensate for them.

9. Negotiate multiple issues simultaneously

An important thing to remember is that when a candidate has more than one demand or 'ask,' they must transparently put them across the table to the company's representative together. In an overwhelming majority of the cases, the representative is not the actual decision maker and will need to reach out to someone else with the 'ask' as well as the basis for the 'ask' and convince someone above them in the hierarchy for a decision for the candidate.

By giving only a few at a time, you not only spend more time in the process for the representative but also lose his/ her advocacy for the position leading to a lower probability of getting a favorable outcome. In one case, the candidate wanted a better salary that matched the grade along with a change of location and a more specific definition of the role. As all the demands were requested in one go, the company considered it positively and agreed to meet all the demands.

10. Don't negotiate just to negotiate

In the case where an offer made by a company is considered suitable by the candidate, he/ she must restrain from negotiating to make it feel as if the company has not met the needs suitably.

Companies do put much effort into making an offer for med-senior laterals, and as such the offers are based on their prior experiences as well as industry benchmarks.

Further, several companies are seen as having either an implicit or explicit 'no negotiations' policy, or clear terms about offers, which they would not move beyond. At times, these are defined in the job descriptions, or a smart candidate can glean the same in the negotiations round as well. The candidate must thus take a very calculated call and decide if negotiating further would push back a company into declining a position.

11. Think through the timing of offers:

At all times and particularly when visiting campuses Companies are observed as making offers to candidates from at least three (if not more) campuses, and as such do calculate their chances of being rejected by a candidate, and prepare for making offers to an alternate candidate from another campus which may be pending for interview/ be in the negotiations stage.

With the limited availability of openings, it becomes crucial to consider the timing of an offer. Candidates often consider very strongly the terms that are explicit, usually monetary, geographical, etc. but a commonly overlooked implicit term is in fact 'Time'. If the negotiations reach a stage where the candidate may be getting an acceptable deal, and the response from the candidate is delayed, it is fairly reasonable to assume that an offer will be made to another candidate, elsewhere, and the current offer may not transpire/ be withdrawn.

At the same time, if the shortlisted candidates undertake immediate acceptance of the offer, it gives a positive impression to the company.

Asking for a reasonable amount of time to make a decision may be valid, but it would be best to ask for 24-48 hours, and no more in most circumstances. There are however some ways of asking for more time, without being obvious about it. Especially when interviewing with a startup, it may be reasonable to ask to speak with the CTO/ CFO/ CMO (primarily a self-initiated additional round of discussion) when at a relatively advanced stage of the negotiation.

This would take some time to set up and conduct, thus buying the candidate the additional time that he/ she requires. Caution: if this extra discussion has not been prepared for well, it can backfire and blow up negatively for the candidate.

12. Avoid, ignore, or downplay ultimatums of any kind

When candidates have a specific 'ask,' they must make an effort to elaborate on the basis of why they feel it is important for them. This is important, especially for criteria such as location. On the basis of the feedback from HR , there are instances where the need has been met, but the way it has been conveyed has not been taken well, and the candidates were already seen in a poor light right at the beginning of the relationship. Further, a candidate must take care not to represent such requirements as ultimatums as it only serves to show the candidate as being inflexible, and unwilling to discuss.

In the opposing case, if a company gives an ultimatum, the candidate must be careful to sidestep and continue the discussion as if it were without the ultimatum, to ensure that the atmosphere of the discussion does not get vitiated and a feasible solution may be found, if not for the present, then for a near-term.

This may mainly be seen to work well with constraints put across by companies such as salaries, other perks, and location specifications. Further, for candidates who seek to make functional or industry shifts, this can come in handy, where the interviewer may state that they seek someone only from a particular background, but the candidate has the knowledge and the capability to fulfill the role under discussion.

13. Remember, they are not out to get you

It is important to know that the recruiter also has a set need, to hire a good candidate. His questions, queries, demeanor may not always reflect that, but the candidate must remember they are not an enemy and are not out to belittle or get you. They simply wish to do the best by their company and fulfill their role, and as such may occasionally push a candidate to check their behavior and response as a part of the process.

For the candidate, such things must be taken in their stride, and patience must be maintained, as the candidate is highly relevant to the interviewer's job. Further, there may be aspects of the negotiation that the interviewer may not be able to give an answer to during the first discussion. In this case, a candidate must seek to gain information about who in the hierarchy may be able to provide the response awaited, and facilitate the interviewer by providing them the necessary information/ time (by suggesting perhaps to meet back again later in the day, allowing space for their internal discussion) and making it clear about the interest and willingness to wait.

This is of course, considering that the requests made are reasonable in nature and the company would be able to fulfill them. Negotiation itself is another round of interview and candidate may be selected or declined based on the discussion during negotiation.

14. Stay at the table

The candidate must always remember, if he walks away from the discussion in any manner, via any signal, even verbal, the further discussion is just moot with no outcome. For constraints that may seem to be insurmountable, it would be a good idea to ask about the best the company can do, and if feasible ask for time to decide.

Keep the interviewers interest open in the candidate and not close the doors completely on the discussion. For terms that seem not entirely acceptable, the candidate would need to put some effort to look for alternative terms which may be improved in lieu as well. Overall, be nice!

15. Maintain a sense of perspective

It is important to have done research beforehand and know enough about the company's/ division's future so that the candidate can genuinely understand the near-term and long-term benefits of the role, as well as ask queries about projected career progression paths.

In the case of startups, it becomes even more pertinent to know about their founder's backgrounds, other interests, source and quantum of funds, current indicative financial and time-to-market positions. This will help to understand the real potential of the role in the company under discussion. In some cases, there would be interviewers with well-set backgrounds in the business, and asking about their growth and experiences can help to refine the perspective well.

Candidates who do this adequately are expected to land roles which allow them to grow well in the chosen path, and not take up a role via placements to only get a job for the sake of income, or job hops after some time.

Selecting an Offer

> *"It is our choices, Harry, that show what we truly are, far more than our abilities."*
>
> **-J K Rowling,**
> *Harry Potter and the Chamber of Secrets*

Like in the case of admits, multiple offers come with the problem of plenty. Still, a better problem to have than to have no offers at whatever stage of your career.

I have faced at least 3 situations in my career where I had more than 2 offers. One of these choices has been easy, and the other two have been gut-wrenching, with multiple logics and emotions to consider. Thankfully, I do not harbor regret over any of these choices.

In the previous section, we learned about how to frame a negotiation using different elements of the offer. Almost all of them can be used to also construct our decision matrix around offers. Job offers, unlike admits tend to be more iterative and incremental, with both parties trying to converge to a zone of possible agreement. Hence, it often gets heady if a structure for considering offers is not already established.

In my framework, the elements of an offer can be divided into categories: tangibles and intangibles. Whereas the tangibles are explicit, the intangibles are implicit and often get ignored when the candidate starts to consider parallel offers. However, a lot of good recruiters make sure that they are selling you on the intangibles as well, especially when they are attempting to lowball you on the salary !

I would recommend that the candidate constructs a table where every single aspect of the offer is tabulated. This helps to track iterative offers from the same firm and also acts as a guide when one aspect of the offer has been missed out by another firm, either deliberately or by mistake.

Note, however, that it is much tougher to compare offers in different countries without also understanding the taxation and the cost of living there and then suitably pairing them with your local currency or the one you are most comfortable with.

Tangible and committed on paper

Cost to Company

The Cost to Company is ubiquitously used by firms everywhere and thoroughly misunderstood by candidates if not using the help of a chartered accountant. Let us attempt to simplify this here. Please note, that this portion will be minimally useful to experienced candidates so they can choose to completely skip it.

The fixed portion: Basic Salary + House Rent Allowance + All other allowances +Medical facilities+ Provident Fund & Gratuity. The key optimizations available here are the following:

- The basic salary is as high as possible within the overall fixed portion. This also increases the employer contribution to the provident fund, provided you choose to avail of the full 12% option from your side. This should be at least as much as your existing salary's basic salary in my opinion. Any offer which

looks to reduce this portion with the promise of increasing elsewhere is for sure to be bargained further with.
- You are able to flexibly allocate much of the allowances, preferably dynamically throughout the fiscal year as you deem relevant to your lifestyle.
- The medical facilities cover you and your family with the added option of topping up the packages as required by you.

The variable portion: Variable pay + Other performance bonuses. I resist adding ESOPs here and will add them in the next segment. I hope that what I mention here helps you to get some relief from the appraisal process and the anxiety surrounding variable pay/bonuses.
- The variable pay portion is commensurate with the role that you perform and your level on the leadership ladder. If you are in an operations role in a middle management role, anything up to 20% is reasonable. If you are offered the role of head of sales in a firm, expect to get an offer which has up to 50-60% of variable pay.
- Make sure that you do not need the variable pay for key necessities like monthly expenses, EMI payments, or big and critical impending purchases. The bonus should be a bonus even after your expenditure is done with and to be earmarked to provide a boost to your savings and investments.
- Continuing with the above, seldom account for receiving anything more than 100% of the variable pay and you will be pleasantly surprised if it happens
- Glassdoor research can yield some information about whether the variable payouts have indeed been honored when both individual and firm have performed

Designation and Span of Control

In my career and that of people around me, I have observed that the misgivings that people experience very early into a new role are as much about designation and span of control as they are about the CTC relative to that of others in the same station.

Particularly, as CAs play around with EBITDA numbers to massage financial reports, HR folks use designations for the same. At the heart of the problem is information asymmetry, the fact that you have limited insight into how the firm's organization is structured. You cannot always count on having a friend or an acquaintance who will be brutally honest about the right designation for you in the firm so public sites like Glassdoor, Ambition Box, and Fishbowl are absolutely critical.

The complexity here is that recruiters often trade off CTC with designation and you might be tempted to bargain for the former at the cost of the latter. I was earlier naive and hence agnostic to designation but now believe that designation, and hence authority is as crucial to your success in a role as are your skills, influence, collaborativeness, conscientiousness, or your perspicacity.

Do not leave the negotiation without fully having expressed and explored the possibility that you getting the right designation fit. Though I do not advocate benchmarking the salaries of other folks during a negotiation process, designations should be benchmarked using Linkedin and explicitly put in front of the recruiters. Better this than having an uncomfortable conversation with your manager and some other HR person, one month into the role.

Tangible and promised verbally

ESOPS

Though ESOPs are of course formally inserted into an offer letter by most firms, I refer to them as just a promise because their value is highly uncertain and volatile.

Unlike other elements of the offer like fixed and variable pay, ESOPs can go boom or bust. Retrospective data has zero utility. How the firm raised money in the last funding cycle and offered a buyback to its employees has no cor relation with what is going to happen in the next cycle.

How do you structure your life around such an uncertainty ? By making sure that they are unnecessary to the equation and at best a pleasant surprise.

Herein lies the problem with evaluating offers between startups, which almost always offer ESOPs, and large companies which rarely do so. In such a situation, the only way a candidate can even consider the startup is similar to the discussion around variable pay, that is the fixed pay or the candidate's earlier savings are more than enough for sustained livelihood and for paying liabilities.

The promise of promotion/ CTC increases

Many, many firms promise incoming candidates that the offer that they are rolling out now is the best that they can do now, with the promise of revising the offer in an upcoming cycle. I have seen such promises being both fulfilled and reneged. The reneging was both for genuine reasons or for the reason that the recruiter was ready to say anything to fill a role and later just didn't bother.

The antidote to this is twofold. Get the promise in writing from the recruiter, even if not in the offer letter (an email should suffice). Then, make sure that the hiring manager (and your reporting manager, if the two are different) receive this written communication preferably before your joining date.

The Intangibles

Reporting Manager

In the section on mentors, I mentioned my experience with reporting managers and how I believe that they can be valued mentors. Here, let me elaborate on their role when considering an offer.

LinkedI n is awash with quotes about how people leave their reporting managers and not their jobs and I believe that there is a great degree of truth in the same. That being said, it is consequential that you consider the reporting manager's personality when you are mulling over an offer. Of course, it is imperative that you talk to the reporting manager not just during the interview but also to be able to gauge him/ her better. Additionally, try to talk to at least 2 people who have also worked in the same team.

In my belief, the things to look out for, during these conversations with a reporting manager are:-

- Does he strike you as not being patronizing or condescending during the interview process itself ?

- Does he encourage and respond comprehensively to questions from you about the ways of working in the team and the firm ?
- Is he open to talk about his life beyond his work ?
- Has he progressed through the ranks and performed the role that has been offered to you ?

The immediate work group

This is the next big influence in the workplace, and the reporting manager plus your team contribute to up to 80% of how you feel about the firm. Look out for similar things in the work- place as you would with a reporting manager. Though it is tough, try to understand the relative reputation of the team within the larger company. Is it a team of achievers or laggards ?

Additionally, understand the composition of the team. Is it full of longtimers in the company who would find it difficult to accommodate an outsider ? Is it full of new joiners, who are collectively grappling with the culture of the place ? Every situation has its own promise and its challenges, and all of these, layered along with what you expect from the workplace help to set the tone for how you will land into the firm and the team.

Location of Work

Location preferences tend to get stronger as one progresses in experience. Sometimes, they are a wow factor, sometimes they are a convenience, and other times, they are a necessity and hence a deal breaker. The latter, particularly for people with a family.

I had joined a firm where the recruiters had packed me off (without a chance of negotiation) to a different place than my city Bengaluru, even though the firm had the largest footprint in Bengaluru. Even my manager and team mates were not sure why I was not back home. Needless to say, my stint there was not long.

Work location matters for two reasons. The first reason is the cost of living. If you have an advantage of being a native, you have an inherent cost advantage compared to migrants to the city. For other places, there are always comparative advantages between the two locations.

The second reason is the networking effect. Bengaluru is good for IT, Pune and Chennai are good for the automotive sector, and so on. This is critical when you are considering your next change !

The Brand

There are situations in your career where you would consider an offer inferior in other parameters, just because of the brand behind the offer. Employer brands have a powerful rub-off on careers, even many many years after you have stopped working for the firm.

The first firm I worked for, right after finishing my undergraduate degree was Toyota. My current manager tells me that he hired me not because of my immediate experience but for my Toyota stint, which in his opinion indicates that I would carry a mindset of keeping the customer first in all my work-based activities. This is more than a decade after I left Toyota, obtained 2 Post graduate degrees, and did stints with 4 other firms in that decade !

It is my strong opinion that though positive brands reflect positively on your profile, negative ones don't impact it a lot.

Even when hiring from dubious firms, employers might still consider candidates who are otherwise considered good, albeit after a much more thorough interview process and a rigorous background check!

Job Offer- Decision Matrix

With a firm understanding of the tangibles and intangibles that go into an offer, you are now ready to evaluate multiple ones. I would recommend that you not consider more than 3 new offers at the same time, as otherwise, you would end up being subjected to analysis paralysis. If more than 3 firms are pursuing you at the same time, it is always ok to communicate to the least desirable firm (from gut instinct, without going into any further negotiations) that you have too many offers to consider and will revert to them at a later time in case you are still available as a candidate.

Additionally, make sure that the first column in your decision matrix is devoted to your current firm and current role. The status quo is also very powerful! However, it is to be noted that many firms try to hold on to candidates by promising salary hikes and promotions at a later point in time. Be sure to consider these promises on par with promises about the future from other offers.

		Scale of 1 to 10, 10 is better			
Parameter	Weightage of Parameter (Adding up to 100%)	Present Role in Present Firm	Offer 1	Offer 2	Offer 3
Tangibles-CTC	25%	3	5	10	1
Tangibles-Designation and Span of Control	10%	7	8	10	10
Tangibles-ESOPs	10%	2	6	6	2
Tangibles-Promises	5%	6	9	3	5
Intangibles-Reporting Manager and Team	25%	9	4	2	10
Intangibles-Location	15%	6	2	1	9
Intangibles-Brand	10%	4	7	7	6
	100%	**5.5**	**5.1**	**5.6**	**6.15**

Conclusion

Thus, we come to the end of this book. With you, the reader having used the concepts and frameworks mentioned here to understand yourself and key stakeholders in the admit and offer process, gain and use the advice of mentors, sell yourself to obtain multiple admits or offers, and then evaluate the most suitable one.

Maybe all of these will not happen in one long chain, and you would have used this book multiple times as the circumstances require. Any way, as long as it works for you.

Let me re-emphasize my key motivations behind writing this book, something which I had mentioned in the chapter on my purpose in writing it.

This book is not my own personal story of personal triumph. I am as confused or as clear about my career, both in hindsight and in foresight as the average person is. However, I can confidently claim to have made peace with my situation and have zero regrets about anything in my career.

This book does not provide the answer to every career-related question that you might have. In fact, it does not even address every unique career choice . Such a book would be beyond my ability as well as would not interest a large, generic audience.

What I have endeavored to do in these pages is to construct mental frameworks that help candidates diligently prepare for careers, ask for the right help at the right time from the right people, and make decisions which are not grossly wrong.

Finally, my definition of success of this book for myself and you is that it helps you to minimize career regret.

Works Cited

MBTIonline: Official Myers Briggs Test & Personality Assessment, https://www.mbtionline.com/. Accessed 16 December 2023.

https://hbr.org/2014/04/15-rules-for-negotiating-a-job-offer.

Boyle, GJ. "Big Five personality traits." *Wikipedia*, https://en.wikipedia.org/wiki/Big_Five_personality_traits. Accessed 16 December 2023.

"College and university rankings." *Wikipedia*, https://en.wikipedia.org/wiki/College_and_university_rankings. Accessed 16 December 2023.

"DISC assessment." *Wikipedia*, https://en.wikipedia.org/wiki/DISC_assessment. Accessed 16 December 2023.

Mishra, Akanksha. "Middle class set to boom in India, avg household income to be Rs 20L/year by 2047, finds PRICE survey." *ThePrint*, 6 July 2023, https://theprint.in/india/middle-class-set-to-boom-in-india-avg-household-income-to-be-rs-20l-year-by-2047-finds-price-survey/1657450/. Accessed 16 December 2023.

Works Cited

M S, Aniruddha. ".," - *YouTube*, 30 October 2023, https://medium.com/me/stats/post/4e1ed12f7b80. Accessed 16 December 2023.

M Visvesvaraya, editor. *Memories Of My Working Life*. HASSELL STREET Press, 2021. Accessed 16 December 2023.

"Myers–Briggs Type Indicator." *Wikipedia*, https://en.wikipedia.org/wiki/Myers%E2%80%93Briggs_Type_Indicator. Accessed 16 December 2023.

"PEST analysis." *Wikipedia*, https://en.wikipedia.org/wiki/PEST_analysis. Accessed 16 December 2023.

"Porter's five forces analysis." *Wikipedia*, https://en.wikipedia.org/wiki/Porter%27s_five_forces_analysis. Accessed 16 December 2023.

Sheikh, Mohsin, and aakanksha chaturvedi. "Infosys, Wipro, TCS: IT CEOs' salary increased 1500% while freshers' salary up only 50% in last 10 years." *Business Today*, 27 December 2022, https://www.businesstoday.in/latest/corporate/story/infosys-wipro-tcs-it-ceos-salary-increased-1500-while-freshers-salary-up-only-50-in-last-10-years-357886-2022-12-27. Accessed 16 December 2023.

"Strong Interest Inventory® | Career test." *The Myers-Briggs Company*, https://www.themyersbriggs.com/en-US/Products-and-Services/Strong. Accessed 16 December 2023.

Sudhaman, KR. "India loses a staggering $80 billion foreign exchange due to students opting to study abroad." *National Herald*, https://

Works Cited

www.nationalheraldindia.com/india/india-loses-a-staggering-80-billion-foreign-exchange-due-to-students-opting-to-study-abroad. Accessed 16 December 2023.

www.ingramcontent.com/pod-product-compliance
Lightning Source LLC
LaVergne TN
LVHW061343080526
838199LV00093B/6926